ST TEATH

A VILLAGE THROUGH TIME

ANNE WORRALL

Contents

Chapter 1 - All roads lead to St Teath   1

Chapter 2 - How it all began   9

Chapter 3 - The Parish Church of St Tetha   20

Chapter 4 - The Celtic Cross   30

Chapter 5 - Anne Jefferies and the Fairies   35

Chapter 6 - The Clock Tower   48

Chapter 7 - Treburgett Mine   53

Chapter 8 - A charismatic Curate   58

Chapter 9 - Chapels   66

Chapter 10 - The Village School   71

Chapter 11 - A Local History Society   83

Chapter 12 - Reminiscences   97

'Of all dull books a conscientiously researched parish history is the dullest.'

Chapter One

All roads lead to St Teath

"There's that place *again*," I said, looking up at the signpost, as my husband stopped the car at a crossroads. "Would you believe it? It seems all roads in North Cornwall lead to this *Saint Teeth* place. I've never heard of it, have you?"

"Sounds like the patron saint of dentists," remarked Fred. He turned the car in the direction of St Teath and added vaguely, "I seem to remember one of those houses for sale was in St Teath. Well, I *think* it was St Teath, everywhere round here seems to be named after some unlikely saint or other."

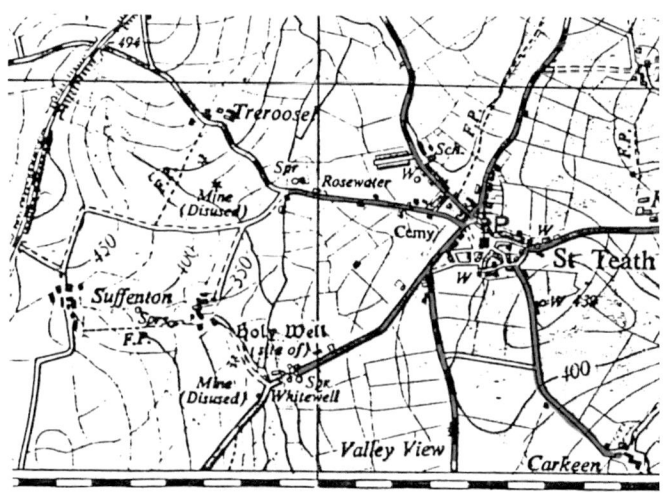

Map from 1900 showing roads into St Teath

"Well, you know what they say - there are more saints in Cornwall than there are in heaven," I reminded him. "Perhaps we could go and have a quick look at this last place before it gets dark, what do you think?"

We drove on for about a mile along a narrow, winding lane with tall hedges on either side. A few minutes later we emerged into a slightly wider road lined with houses. The buildings were a hotchpotch of old stone cottages, suburban semis, bungalows and even a small block of flats. It looked as if someone had tried to put together as many examples of different styles of architecture as they could fit into the short lane. After only about a hundred yards Fred drew up at yet another junction. He wound down the window and beheld a rather grim-looking Methodist chapel on the corner, its notice board boldly proclaiming: *JESUS IS ALIVE TODAY*!

"It looks as if He might be the only person round here who is," commented Fred, looking at the deserted streets. "But didn't we just pass another chapel only a few yards back?"

"Yup, and there's a church in front of us," I announced, peering through the windscreen into the gathering gloom. "People's spiritual needs are certainly well catered for here."

"More to the point there's a decent-looking pub : *The White Hart Inn, Good Beer, Good Food,*" Fred read the board on an old, whitewashed, stone building, then added, "Pity, it's closed."

I shuffled through the reams of paper that the estate agent had pressed into our hands. The poor man had greeted our arrival in his Wadebridge office with unbounded joy, making us feel very guilty, since we had only gone inside to get out of the bitterly cold wind and snow showers. The weather this Easter holiday had been dreadful with arctic temperatures, blizzards and gales. It was definitely not the sort of weather for walking or sitting on the beach, even for the hardiest of holidaymakers which my family most certainly were not. Cornwall in 1975 did not offer a lot in the way of entertainment during inclement weather. Comparing house prices and nosing around other people's homes had seemed an entertaining way of passing the time until lunch.

"Have you any properties for sale within about ten miles of here?" Fred had asked, not wishing to venture too far in the icy conditions.

"Only about four hundred!" the man had replied, leaping up to the filing cabinet and pulling out dozens of printed sheets. The property market had taken a sudden turn for the worse during the previous year. No one was buying and the house prices printed at the top of the schedules had been crossed out and reduced several times.

"'Tis 'zackly the right time to buy!" the man had enthused handing over a jangle of keys each with an address label attached. "Oh, it's all right, the houses are all empty," he added, seeing our surprised faces. "You can view them at your leisure. Just bring the keys back before

5 o'clock - or put them through the letterbox if we're closed."

"What fun!" I had thought. The prospect of poking around other people's houses with no one to supervise us was an enticing one which promised all kinds of excitement. And so it had proved. We spent a fascinating day exploring every kind of property from tiny dolls' house cottages, with rooms so small there would not have been space for a three-seater sofa, to rambling, windswept farmhouses with breath-taking views of the wild, storm-tossed sea. Gradually and almost imperceptibly the crazy idea that maybe, just maybe, we could drop everything and move from our home in London to what had always been for us just an idyllic holiday location began to plant itself in our minds.

Whenever we had made the overnight journey down from London, as we had done regularly each Spring and Autumn for several years, the moment when we crossed the Tamar into Cornwall had always meant for me entry into a different country, an unreal sort of place, a land of legend. Cornwall was the setting for Daphne du Maurier's tales of smugglers and wreckers, a timeless region, somehow isolated from the mundane world of work and shopping and day-to-day living. The idea that ordinary people like us with jobs and mortgages and young children could live permanently in such a beautiful, mystical place had never crossed our minds – until that day.

I groped around on the floor of the car and picked up a couple of closely typed sheets of paper.

"Ah, here's the one you were thinking of," I said, "There's no photo, it just says *'a detached, modernised country cottage with large garden and garage in a pleasant position on the outskirts of the pretty village of St Teath.'* Pretty village! We've obviously missed something. Let's do a quick tour of the village and then go and have a look at this one last place, before we head back to the hotel. What do you say?"

"Okay," sighed Fred, looking at his watch. "So which way's the centre of the village, do you think – left, right or straight ahead?"

"Let's try left, that seems to be where all the shops are."

On one side of the street we passed a sweetshop, optimistically offering ice cream and a Post Office with a startling selection of goods for sale in the window, including iced cakes, a mop and bucket and some ladies' vests. On the opposite side of the street was a small newsagent's shop with a window full of vegetables. A few yellowing newspapers clung tenaciously to a rusty rack which squeaked back and forth in the biting wind. Next came a red telephone box, a few more old cottages, Victorian villas and pebble-dashed bungalows, a short, tree-lined hill and then suddenly we were at a junction with the main A39 road and a sign pointing back to *'St Teath ½ mile'*.

"Obviously not this way," muttered Fred and turned the car round.

We retraced our short route back to the newsagent's and carried straight on, past a Clock Tower, an abandoned Coop store, a butcher's shop, a few more cottages, a small, tin-roofed garage with one petrol pump, the village school – and a circular end-of-speed-restriction sign marking the end of the village.

"Obviously not this way either," grumbled a scowling Fred, as he turned the car round once again.

"Are we there yet?" came a plaintive cry from the backseat, where our 6-year old and her baby sister were getting restive.

"Not long now," I reassured the children. "It has to be down there," I told my husband, with more certainty than I felt, pointing towards the only unexplored road that remained, leading between the churchyard and the tall Clock Tower. A cemetery, half a dozen cottages and a few trees further down the lane we encountered the de-restriction traffic sign again. Fred stopped the car and folded his arms.

"Well," he said sarcastically, "you can certainly see why all the roads lead here. This place is definitely a hub of activity."

"There are some really nice old cottages – and it's very quiet," I murmured rather lamely.

"You don't normally have umpteen roads leading to a place, because it's rather *quiet*," retorted Fred with undeniable logic.

I gazed at the high hedges which once more blocked our view of the surrounding countryside and then looked up at the signpost and back at the sheet of paper on my lap.

"Look, we're on the road to Pendoggett. It says here that this cottage is *'on the outskirts of St Teath on the road that leads to Pendoggett.'* We might just as well have a look at it, since we're so close."

Perhaps it was the grass growing through the uneven slate floor in the parlour; perhaps it was the moss adorning the inside of all the sash windows and sills; perhaps it was the towering nettles and clinging brambles which made the approach to the house all but impassable, or perhaps it was just the feeling of total neglect and desolation which hung over this little cottage, but something clearly touched our hearts and possibly our brains, dispelling all vestiges of common-sense. We drove back to the estate agent's and put in an offer on the cottage.

Just three short months later we found ourselves with one small child and a baby, sitting on packing cases, surrounded by all our worldly goods in the middle of a cold, dank, cobweb-festooned room in this run-down, old cottage, wondering what on earth we had done. What was it about this place that had made a normally rational, cautious and above all sensible person like me agree to the reckless plan to sell a perfectly good, centrally-heated semi with fitted carpets in every room, give up the best, most rewarding job in the world, leave bewildered friends and family and move into this damp, dilapidated Cornish cottage in the middle of nowhere?

Chapter Two

Where it all began

In those first few months it often felt as if we had travelled back in time to a pre-war era when life was simpler, more straight-forward and very much more basic. Our only heating came from the log fire which we kept burning constantly in the huge, open fireplace in an attempt to get rid of the damp, musty atmosphere that pervaded every corner of the cottage on even the sunniest days.

I gave the children their evening baths on the hearth in front of the blazing fire with towels draped over a wooden clotheshorse, just as my mother had done when I was a child in the forties. We then toasted crumpets on long forks as close to the glowing embers as we dared without burning our knuckles. Domestic chores had never been among my favourite activities, but I nevertheless took an unexpected pleasure in chopping wood and gathering kindling to light the fires, as well as black-leading the grates and the ends of my fingers to a dull, black shine with Zebo polish.

There was an ancient, primitive central-heating system, consisting of a rusty, oil-fuelled boiler, situated in an old fireplace at one end of the parlour, linked to two radiators, one in a fairly normal position in the front room and the other halfway up the wall in the parlour.

"Must be something to do with gravity," Fred had explained, when I asked why this radiator was suspended like an unlovely work of art about a foot from the ceiling. When neither the force of gravity nor Fred's unstinting efforts could persuade the boiler to work, he disconnected the pipes and threw the boiler together with the two radiators out into the garden, where they immediately disappeared from view amongst the tall grass, nettles and weeds.

The children spent most of their time outside in this wilderness, since even on the coolest days it always felt warmer out there than in the cottage, where the thick walls and small windows prevented any of the sun's rays from penetrating the interior. The grass and nettles waved about far above the head of Tanya, our six-year-old daughter. Clouds of grass seeds and insects rose every time a patch of vegetation was disturbed to erect the baby, Tasha's playpen. But the trees were wonderful for climbing and already showed signs of producing a bewildering number of different varieties of apples.

Our neighbours in the lane and on the farm were friendly, helpful and very patient with these townies who had arrived as if from another planet to live in their midst. Although my husband and I had both been born in rural areas, we had spent the last fifteen years, most of our adult lives, in cities and were complete novices when it came to country living. I fortunately resisted the urge to ring the farmer during a heavy downpour one evening to remind him his cows were getting wet out in the field behind our cottage, but we must nevertheless have provided villagers with a fair amount of entertainment with the things we said and did in those early days.

There were, however, some aspects of rural life that came as a disappointment to me. I was dismayed to learn that the farmer next door was not allowed to sell me milk, despite leaving his large, metal churns at the bottom of the drive outside my gate each morning for the tanker to collect.

I could remember as a child holding out jugs and bowls for the milkman to fill with milk ladled out of similar churns which stood in the back of a horse-drawn cart. Milk delivered to the doorstep in glass bottles by Sam, the Unigate man, did not fit my romantic vision of Cornish country living. I had also envisaged buying butter from a rosy-cheeked farmer's wife who had spent all day churning it in a barrel, but instead I had to purchase it in silver packets from the village shop the same as everyone else in St Teath.

Although mains water had arrived in St Teath back in 1937, our cottage, together with the others in the lane, was not connected to the mains supply and still had its own well and sewerage system. The water was pumped very efficiently from the spring-fed well at the bottom of the garden to the house by means of an electric pump. When there was a bad storm with strong winds, as happened frequently in the winter months, the cable carrying the electricity down the lane on shaky poles would often be blown down. This caused power-cuts leaving everyone in the lane without electricity, sometimes for days on end. No electricity meant no power to the pump, so there was no water either.

On these mornings I took my bucket and kettle and walked up the lane to the spring on the side of the road. I had learned from our neighbour, dear old Mrs Cocks, that this was once the holy well which had given the hamlet of Whitewell its name. (*Gwyn* in Cornish means both 'white' and 'holy'). It used to be a stone-built well with a pump and villagers would come down with their pails for the fresh water, which now simply gushed out of a pipe in the wall. Frost glistened all around and steam swirled up from the stream, as I stood waiting for the bucket to fill. I looked down at the old, moss-covered stones on to which the water had splashed for centuries and thought of all the people in the past who had carried water from that same spring. There would certainly have been girls in Victorian times wearing high buttoned boots and long dresses which trailed in the mud, perhaps people even as far back as Tudor times? I had no idea how old our cottage or the others in the hamlet were, but I was eager to find out.

We gradually settled into village life and soon learnt how to pronounce 'St Teath' properly, as demonstrated by the old rhyme:

If one should chance to have a wreath,
You should not take it to St Teath,
For only in the case of death
Should wreaths be taken to St Teath.

I got to know a great deal about life in the village in days gone by from Mrs Cocks in the cottage next door. We spent many happy afternoons sitting in front of her old, black range, drinking tea from pretty china cups with sooty fingerprints round the edges and listening to her tales of St Teath when she was a child. Another elderly neighbour from the 500-year-old farm behind our cottage called in from time to time with yet more fascinating stories about the characters who had once lived in our house and about happenings in the village many years ago. It seemed the past was all around us, mingling with the present and giving a sense of stability and permanence, which I found comforting and reassuring in our fast-moving and ever-changing world.

The more familiar I became with this place that had become my home the more I wanted to know about its history. When and where did it all begin? Who was St Teath, this mysterious saint? And why were there so many roads, one of which fortunately brought us here, leading into this small Cornish village? I was sure the answers to these and many more questions were waiting to be discovered in books - there was no internet in those days - and so began a long and hugely enjoyable journey into the village's past. Hours of poring over reference books in the local history section of nearby Camelford library, often with Tasha, the baby, obligingly asleep in her carry cot and Marie, the friendly librarian ready to give her a cuddle if she woke up, gradually revealed the following remarkable story:

It had all begun an incredible 1,500 years ago in South Wales where the legendary Welsh Prince, Brychan had married long-suffering Gladys who went on to bear him twenty-four children. Brychan had been born in Ireland and had been converted to Christianity there, so as soon as his children were old enough he sent them out into the world as missionaries to convert the country's pagans. North Cornwall was on an established trading route at that time from Wales to Brittany, so it was along this road that the daughters of Brychan travelled to fulfil their religious mission. These young women are remembered in the names of many villages in this area, among them: Mabena (St Mabyn), Adwena (Advent), Endelienta (St Endellion), Morwenna (Morwenstow), Menfreda (St Minver) and, of course, Tetha, our own St Teath.

The almost circular shape of St Teath's present churchyard suggests that this was already an ancient site sacred to the Celts when Tetha chose this particular spot to start her evangelising. Here she built an oratory, a small chapel for prayer and worship. It was common practice for the first Christian churches to be built on sites previously associated with the old pagan religions, as it made it easier for people to accept conversion from their former Celtic belief in the gods of nature and to adopt the Christian faith. The Celtic cross, which now stands in the cemetery across the road from the churchyard, is far too tall and intricately decorated to have been simply a wayside cross, so was clearly the original churchyard cross. (You can read the story of this beleaguered monument's chequered past in Chapter 4). The original base of the cross, discovered near the south door of our present church, shows that this is where the entrance to Tetha's oratory must also have been. This would indicate that the villagers of St Teath have prayed and worshipped on this very same piece of ground for nearly two thousand years - an awe-inspiring thought.

St Teath in the 1940s, showing the circular site of the church and churchyard.

Nothing remains of Tetha's oratory, which was probably a rather flimsy wattle and daub structure. This would have been replaced over time by a Saxon church. These were usually wooden buildings which were unable to survive the ravages of the Cornish climate. However, remnants of the Norman church which followed can be seen both inside the present church building and in garden walls around the village. Ever-resourceful St Teath villagers took advantage of the ambitious rebuilding of the church in the mid-1300s and claimed bits of discarded Norman masonry for use in their own building projects. These remnants are still to be found in gateposts and walls around the village, most obviously in the roadside wall of Garden Cottage on Fore Street, (on the left as you enter the centre of the village from Knights Mill,) where entire windows have been incorporated into the wall.

The priest at this time clearly shared his parishioners' resourcefulness. The original Norman font, which now stands on the floor in the back of the church, was discovered in 1976, to great rejoicing, buried in a field outside the present Vicarage Farm. Situated a mile outside the village and mid-way between St Teath and Delabole, this was the official church vicarage from Norman times until 1821 when the imposing Old Vicarage next to St Teath church was built. Showing great inventiveness, if a certain lack of respect for this ancient relic, the priest had made holes in each side of the sandstone font for the water to go in and out, so that it could be used as a washbasin in the vicarage stream. This ancient font now stands on the floor at the North West end of the church, close to other remains of the Norman building between the last pillar and the belfry. The only other Norman relics are the capitals which support the slate altar in the Lady Chapel. The 'new' hexagonal font, situated at the north end of the church, is made of Tintagel greenstone and has been in constant use for baptisms since its installation in 1380 and has lock holes on each side of the lid to prevent the Holy Water from being stolen.

Most of St Teath's present day church building dates from this period in the mid to late 1300s. About a century before this, in the mid1200s, Bishop Bronscombe had founded two prebends in the church, making it collegiate. It had thus become the most important church in the area. This was at the time when the Black Death was wreaking havoc across the whole country and devastating entire communities. Possibly as much as a third of the population of the country was wiped out during this time. Such a catastrophe brought about a cult of the dead and prayers for the souls of the deceased took on an even greater importance. Religious belief stressed the necessity of preparing for death and the afterlife. The Catholic doctrine defines Purgatory as the place where our soul goes after death and where it is made to suffer to atone for the sins committed in life. It is only when all our sins have been purged that our soul can be received into Heaven. A document from the 14th century in Exeter Cathedral invites the faithful to make a pilgrimage to St Teath to obtain remission on the length of time their souls will be condemned to spend in Purgatory. Moreover, in the will of a certain Sir William Bonevylle in 1408 there is reference to a legacy of twenty shillings *'al heremyte de Sttetth pour prier pour moi'* ('to the hermit of St Teath to pray for me') suggesting that there was a recognised hermitage in the parish at this time. It is perhaps to this shrine that pilgrims were being exhorted to travel to improve their chances in the afterlife.

The church was at the very centre of mediaeval life, as a venue not only for prayer and worship, baptisms, marriages and funerals but also for entertainment, plays and feasting. People would walk to the church from the outlying hamlets and farmsteads several times a week to attend services, gatherings and festivities of all kinds. In addition, as we have learnt, pilgrims would also be making the journey to St Teath from all over the county and beyond for the good of their souls. This network of ancient, well-trodden footpaths into St Teath has become today's plethora of roads, as a glance at any map will show. It has to be said that most of these roads are to this day more suited to walkers and pilgrims than to today's speeding traffic.

The more I delved into the past, the clearer it became that many answers to fundamental questions about the history of this village lay in the history of its oldest building, the church. The major role played by St Teath church in all aspects of community life from its origins to the present day makes it the village's strongest link with the past. I needed to become better acquainted with this beautiful, old building.

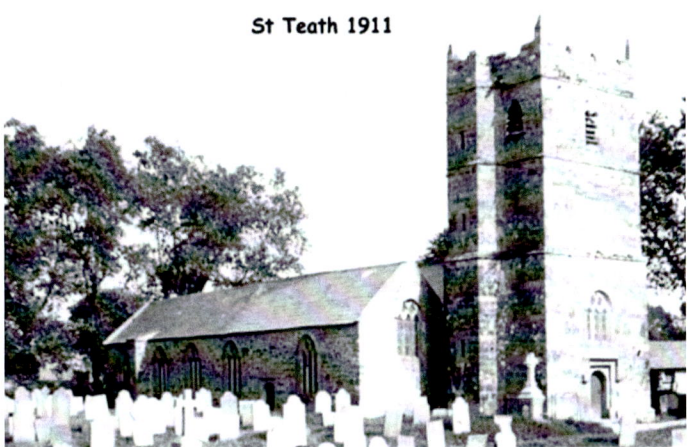

St Teath 1911

Chapter Three

The Parish Church of St Tetha

As you lift the heavy iron latch and push open the solid oak door into St Teath church, you become immediately aware of a profound sense of calm and peacefulness. The vast span of history that this building has witnessed is almost too much to take in. Looking round at the ancient stone walls and granite pillars, it is deeply moving to think of the generations of people who have stood on this spot and touched these very stones. People all those centuries ago suffering the tragic effects of the Black Death, people in the reign of Henry VIII trying to make sense of his religious reforms, people in Elizabeth's reign fearing a possible invasion by the Spanish Armada, people praying for the King in the Civil War and shocked by the violence of the iconoclasts under Cromwell, people struggling to feed their families and fearing the workhouse in the Victorian era, people praying for their husbands and sons in two World Wars, all these people walked through that very same door into the ambience of peace and knelt in prayer on the same slate floor. Standing in this ancient building, it becomes impossible to think of these people as mere characters from the pages of a history textbook, they become real, living people. Here the links with the past are strong and tangible.

Almost all the building we see today dates from the 14th century, around the time when Richard II was on the throne and fighting the Hundred Years War against France. If we step back in time over 600 years and imagine ourselves in the church when it was first built, we can look up at the vine-decorated moulding and bosses high on the side walls and on the ceiling of the north and south aisles and envisage them as they were when freshly carved. At this time, before the Victorian restoration, they would also have also adorned the ceiling of the nave. The carvings are of the original oak, which has miraculously survived the damp Cornish climate. Some of this woodwork, removed from the ceiling of the nave during the restoration, now decorates the side walls of the porch.

The walls would have been covered with paintings of scenes from the Bible and vivid depictions of the torments of Hell. The narrow, winding staircase next to the Lady Chapel, now apparently leading into thin air, originally led onto what was known as the Rood Beam. This was a narrow walkway stretching across the Chancel above the Rood Screen which separated the Sanctuary with its sacred altar from the rest of the church. In mediaeval times the priest would stand high on the beam and declaim his exhortations to the congregation to obey God's commandments or risk the fiery flames of Hell. It is easy to imagine the terror he would have struck into the hearts of those standing before and below him. The congregation would all have been standing, since the only seating at this time was a bench along the side wall of the church for the disabled and those too old and infirm to stand - the weakest went to the wall. Beneath the floor of the church would be the graves of the lords of the manor and eminent personages, often with stone effigies adorning them.

Pews were introduced about a hundred years later when priests' sermons got longer and the congregation's attention span shorter. The carved bench-ends in the north and south aisles are from this time and show a mixture of Christian symbols, coats of arms and pagan figures. Clearly discernible are an altar cross and instruments of the crucifixion; there is also, among others, the Arms of the Fitzjames family showing a dolphin, surrounded by small circles, which is the alchemists' symbol for gold; on another bench is what appears to be a Green Man. All the lords and wealthy parishioners would have had their own personal pews, exclusively for their family's use. These would often have had gates which could be locked to keep out the lower orders. The pews in the nave were removed and replaced by chairs during the Victorian restoration. The bench-ends from these central pews were inexplicably spirited away at this time to Tintagel church where they were joined together to make a screen which was then placed behind the altar and which can still be seen there to this day. Perhaps a campaign should be launched, on the lines of the Greek demand for the return of the Elgin Marbles, for the return of the St Teath Bench-Ends?

Once seating was introduced into the church, there was no longer space for social gatherings such as plays, funeral wakes or feasting, all of which had previously taken place in the church itself. Accordingly separate buildings known as Church Houses were built and St Teath's present Community Centre is a rare example of such a building which has survived virtually in its original state to the present day. A survey in the 1980s by people who know about these things explained that the substantial timber used in the heavy ceiling beams indicate that the building dates from the very early 1500s - the mullion window on the ground floor is also from this time.

The main use of Church Houses was for brewing ale and baking for feast days and wakes. There is evidence of a former partition originally dividing the ground floor into two rooms: a large room on the left and a smaller service room on the right. A blocked entrance on the back wall would have given direct access from the churchyard, when the level of the ground was much lower. When Cromwell and the Puritans banned the brewing and consumption of ale in the mid 1600s many Church Houses fell into ruin or were used for other purposes. There is evidence that the upper floor of our building was used as a Dame School, a small private school presided over by a School Mistress, Later the ground floor of the building became a workhouse for the parish poor and it is likely that the two fireplaces were added at this time.

In the early 1900s the ground floor was reputedly used as a home for unmarried mothers, it then became a Men's Institute (numerous certificates for cock-fighting festooned the beams until quite recently). A carpenter had his workshop there and the village barber plied his trade, among others. By the time we arrived in St Teath in the 70s, the first floor was being used as a billiard room but the ground floor had fallen into disuse and the whole building was in a state of disrepair. In 1985, however, a group of village builders, carpenters and labourers got together and voluntarily spent evenings and weekends for months repairing and restoring the building, so that villagers could once more use it for the purpose for which it was originally intended, as a place to meet for social events and feasting of all kinds. It is heart-warming to think of people in the reign of the first Elizabeth enjoying the company of friends within these same walls – though unfortunately all that is brewed there these days is tea.

If we now return to the church building itself in mediaeval times, the stone effigy which occupies the window-sill in the south aisle nearest to the organ, would have originally been on the under-floor grave of this renowned 15th century knight. However, when pews were installed the effigy would clearly have been in the way and was unceremoniously removed to its present resting place on the windowsill, to the frustration of today's flower arrangers who are at a loss to find somewhere to stand a vase. Now looking very much the worse for wear, our knight looked far more dapper when the historian, Sir John Maclean visited the church in 1868. He described the knight as having *'the head supported by angels and at the feet two lions. The figure is clad in a shirt, painted red, and over this about the neck is a knotted cord from which is suspended an ornament of a quatrefoil form. The vesture falls in graceful folds to near the ankle and painted amber colour. The hair is of a rich brown, without a tonsure, but parted in the middle and having short crisp curls all around. '* If a knight died peacefully at home, his effigy was carved showing his feet resting on a little dog, but if he died in battle his feet rested on the body of a lion. The St Teath knight evidently died in battle and the style of his hair and clothes places him firmly in the 1400s. This is the period of the Battle of Agincourt, so it seems at least possible that this may have been where our unknown knight met his death.

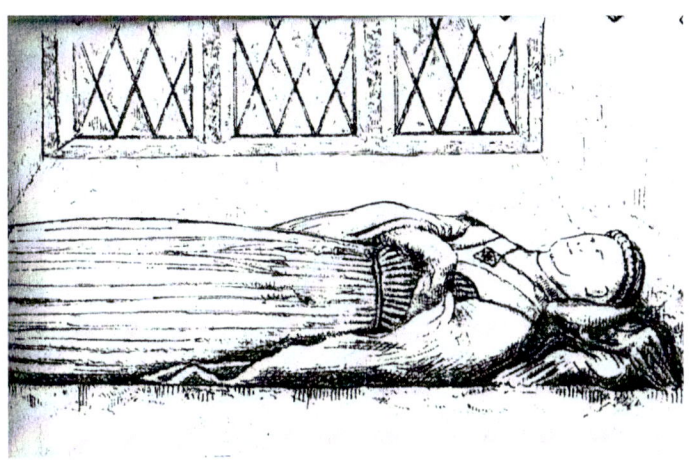

The early 1600s saw the extension of the tower to house the belfry - the year 1630 can be seen engraved over the external door of the tower. This extension was paid for by William Carminow, who lived in Trehannick Manor (on the road leading from Trehannick Sawmills to St Teath) and who was a well-known supporter of the Royalist cause and of the Catholic religion. He was attacked and his house ransacked by a mob of Parliamentarians in 1646 and he died later that year, the last of the Carminow line. The pulpit is of this period and bears the arms of the Carminow family with the cryptic motto *'Cala Rag Whetlow'*, which translates as 'A Straw for a Tale-bearer'. The story goes that in the 14th century one of the Carminow family, who claimed descent from King Arthur, was called upon to prove his right to bear the simple Arms - a blue shield with a diagonal band. Two other English knights, Scrope and Grosvenor also claimed these Arms and the case went to court, resulting in Scrope being granted the right to retain the Arms. Carminow maintained that his Arms had been granted to the family by King Arthur himself centuries before and so he too was allowed to bear the arms. Presumably Scrope, a name worthy of a Dickensian villain, is the person referred to as the 'Tale-bearer'.

The overthrow of the monarchy and rise of the Puritans brought about incalculable damage to churches at that time. The Puritans with their strict beliefs regarded all statues and imagery as icons of idolatry and superstition, and mobs of iconoclasts went around destroying sculptures, paintings and windows. Most of our church's stained glass windows were smashed at this time. The east window over the altar contains a circular fragment of the original glass depicting the Passion with Christ's heart transfixed by a spear and his hands and feet pierced by nails. There are also a few isolated fragments of original glass which were dug up from the ground under the windows in the churchyard during Victorian times and replaced in the upper lights of windows on the south side of the church. Also during the Reformation the considerable treasures of what was such an important church were plundered. Just inside the south door is the sole remaining artefact of the Jacobean period, an Alms box, with stout metal hinges and, now just about visible, painted figures round the sides together with the inscription, *'Remember the Poor.'*

At the back of the church against the wall are three tomb slabs which would have originally been on graves under the floor in the body of the church. The largest of these, a slate slab, 6ft high, is a beautifully engraved memorial to Frances Bennet who died in 1636. It depicts Frances Bennet in the elaborate dress of the period, holding a skull in her left hand and a prayer book in her right and with two small figures of children. The inscription around the border reads: *Here lyeth the body of Franncis the wife of Phillipe Bennet of this parissh who was buried the .... day of October Anno Domini 1636.* On the wall of the belfry is what is considered to be the oldest slate memorial in existence anywhere today. It shows a simple Latin cross with the following inscription: *Heare lieth the bodi of John Taverner, Gentel and too sonnes and too daughters buried 3rd December Anno Domini 1586.* Spelling in those days appears to have been somewhat haphazard.

    St Teath boasts its original Parish Records, the oldest in the county, which date back to 1558, the year in which Elizabeth I decreed that records of all baptisms, marriages and burials within the parish should be kept by the church. I like to think that it is St Teath's special feeling of respect for the past that has ensured that these records have survived when those of so many other parishes have been lost. The original register with its wooden covers and leather binding, containing all entries from 1558 to 1721, was kept in St Teath church until 1996 when a new vicar was persuaded to allow it to be removed to the Cornwall Record Office in Truro for safe-keeping. Despite receiving many pleas on behalf of the Record Office, the previous vicar, Rev Michael Pearce had adamantly refused to allow the register to leave St Teath church, insisting that this was where it belonged.

    In Rev Pearce's time, it was thrilling to be allowed to don cotton gloves and handle this precious volume with its beautifully calligraphed names, but it was worrying to see how it was showing its age. The parchment had become discoloured, creased and torn in places and was clearly in need of the special care and protection it is now receiving. A transcript of the entire register remains in the village. It is astonishing how many of the names which appear in the 1500s, at that time spelt in weird and wonderful ways, occur time after time throughout the ages and continue to be familiar names in the village today. These families, going back almost twenty generations, only serve to emphasise the way in which St Teath's history constantly bridges the centuries to form living connections with its far distant past.

Chapter Four

The Celtic Cross

As a relic from St Teath's far distant past and the oldest monument in the village, the ancient Celtic cross standing at the entrance to the cemetery has not always been granted the respect it deserves. Why does it now stand in the cemetery instead of at the entrance to the church where it was meant to be? And why are there what appear to be several joins in its tall granite shaft?

A chance meeting one morning in the Square with a representative of English Heritage, who was conducting a survey of Cornish crosses, provided answers to many of my questions and revealed a sorry tale of neglect and deliberate mutilation, culminating in what she described as *'by far the worst example of wanton vandalism ever recorded to a Cornish stone cross'*.

With the help of Arthur Langdon's book, *'Old Cornish Crosses'*, I was able to piece together the unhappy history of this granite monolith, which at 13 ft is officially the third tallest cross in Cornwall. Mylor's cross is indisputably the tallest at 17ft, but the one at Quethiock, which claims to be second tallest, is a mere 4 inches taller than St Teath's.

I maintain that our cross is in fact the second tallest in Cornwall, since 8 inches of its shaft had to be sunk into its present base due to the original tenon being broken off, as we shall see.

Arthur Langdon refers to the original empty cross base still being in the churchyard when he was writing in 1893. This was obviously where the cross had stood until smashed off its base and pulled down, most probably by the Puritan reformists during the Reformation. It lay on the ground where it fell at the entrance to the church until it was eventually dragged a few yards to be used as a lowly footbridge over a pool of water outside what is now Forge Cottage. This was to be its fate for the next two hundred years.

In 1835 Rev Joseph Fayrer recognised the cross for the sacred monument it was. He had it lifted from this ignominious position and returned to the churchyard, intending to re-erect it on its original base by the south door but he encountered huge problems. The tenon had been broken off the shaft and the base stone had been badly damaged over the years. Rev Fayrer started work on the repairs but unfortunately died, aged only 52, before he could complete the task. A headstone to his memory stands outside the south door to the church, close to the spot where the cross would have originally stood. The Rev Thomas Amory succeeded Rev Fayrer but unfortunately did not share his predecessor's respect for this historic monument and saw it more as a god-given supply of building materials. The head of the cross was broken off and smashed into two pieces, so that a large part of it could be used as a pivot for the churchyard gate. The long shaft itself was then chopped in half and the upper half cut into blocks to be used in the building of a wall for the churchyard. The lower half was split lengthways, smoothed to erase the ancient decoration and one edge chamfered to be used as coping for the wall.

The mutilated parts of the cross remained in the wall for over forty years until in 1883 Rev Thomas Worthington identified the disparate sections and heroically came to the cross's rescue. He had the fragments removed from the wall, bolted the two halves of the lower part of the shaft together and cemented the cubes of the upper half on to it. The only part of the head he could find was that being used as a pivot, so a stonemason was given the task of filling in the large gaping hole on the upper left-hand side. This he did using pieces of red brick covered with mortar and he then cemented the head onto the shaft. Why Rev Worthington chose to re-erect the restored cross in the recently-opened cemetery rather than in the churchyard is not known, although it is possible that he did not wish to disturb any burials that had taken place in the meantime. With the top stone from an old Epping Stock (steps used by riders to mount a horse) as a new base, the cross has now been standing proudly in its present position for well over a hundred years.

In the 1980s when I was researching the cross's history it was clear that the stonemason's ad hoc repairs, which had withstood more than a century of Cornish weather, were beginning to show the ravages of time. The mortar covering the pieces of brick, used to replace the missing section of the head, had begun to fall away leaving the red bricks exposed and several holes were clearly visible. Fortunately in 1995 North Cornwall Heritage Coast & Countryside Service in conjunction with English Heritage put together a restoration project to rebuild the missing part of the head and protect the cross from deteriorating further.

Expertly restored, the cross now stands proud, as evidence of the village's deep roots in the far distant past. This ancient cross appears on vestments worn in church services. Furthermore, when many years later, as Chair of governors for the village school, I was asked to suggest a logo for the school badge, I could think of no better symbol of St Teath's long history than this iconic and supremely resilient Celtic cross.

Chapter Five

Anne Jefferies and the Fairies

With the start of the school year our life settled into a routine of morning walks up the hill to take Tanya to the village school, pushing Tasha in an enormous, four-wheeled pram of the kind in which all babies travelled in those laborious, pre-buggy days. The air was clear and fresh and Tanya enjoyed giving the horses in the fields that we passed a friendly pat on the head each morning. We also collected acorns to feed to the pigs in the field next to the village school. It was a different world from our West London suburban life with its daily commute to school and work in heavy traffic.

People soon began to stop and chat as I made my daily visit to the shop for food and to collect the newspaper and I became used to the unhurried, easy-going way of village life, where popping into the shop for one item could often take anything up to an hour. As I stood chatting with a group of villagers in the newsagent's one spring morning, a holidaymaker rushed in holding a newspaper from the rack outside. He hopped impatiently from one foot to the other for a few minutes, whilst the shopkeeper and a customer argued the merits of putting electric lights in chicken coops, then he pushed forward to the counter holding out his money.

"I'm sorry, I've got a bus to catch!" he explained, handing over the coins.

Mr Spry, the shopkeeper ignored the money and shook his head pityingly.

"You'll find buses don't go that fast round 'ere, me 'ansome," he informed the nonplussed commuter, "Nor nothing else neither," he added, before continuing his important chicken coop discussion. It was indeed a different world.

With my newspaper and shopping finally tucked under the covers of the pram, I went for a stroll in the morning sunshine around the oldest part of the village known as the 'island': the group of 16th and 17th century cottages huddled together on the edge of the churchyard. As I struggled to push the pram over the uneven ground, three children on bikes pedalled past, shouting and laughing. Just in front of us the girl who was leading them suddenly stopped with her front wheel stuck in the gap between two paving stones.

"Come on, Em!" the older boy shouted, overtaking her. "Don't stop there! That place is creepy." He pointed to one of a terrace of old stone cottages.

"What do you mean, 'creepy'?" the younger boy called out nervously, pedalling hard to catch up.

"My Gran says it's haunted, she says *a witch* used to live there," the other boy shouted back over his shoulder in dramatic tones.

"*Your Gran* says telephones are the work of the devil," the girl scoffed, yanking her wheel free and getting back on her bike. "She also says Plymouth Argyle will win the cup," she added scornfully.

"Witches roast little boys in the oven," the boy yelled back to the wide-eyed little boy. "You'd better watch out, Darren!"

The girl started to cycle off, as Darren caught her up. "Don't worry Darren, I've heard she was a good witch. They say she used to talk to fairies and do magic and stuff like that."

She cycled off after the older boy, with Darren bringing up the rear and pedalling as hard as he could. As they headed off round the corner, I heard the older boy's voice as it faded into the distance, "And if you believe that, you'll believe anything..."

I was intrigued. For the next few weeks I spent every spare moment in the local library in Camelford. I was searching for any scrap of information about this so-called St Teath 'witch'. Where did the story come from? Could there be any truth in it?

Gradually I pieced together a few different versions of this strange tale. Some, including one of the most detailed, by Robert Hunt in 1891, clearly owed more to a fertile imagination than to historical fact. However, one unbelievably exciting day I came across a book entitled *Cornish Characters and Strange Events* by Baring-Gould, published in 1908. In it I was thrilled to find an entire chapter devoted to *Anne Jefferies*. I had found the St Teath 'witch'. There followed a word-for-word copy of a letter, written in 1696 by Moses Pitt, a London publisher, to the Bishop of Gloucester, who was known for his interest in the supernatural. It transpired that Moses Pitt had been born in St Teath and Anne Jefferies had worked as a servant for his family, looking after Moses when he was a young boy. The letter was a detailed personal account of all he remembered of the extraordinary events involving Anne, the so-called 'witch'. After unsuccessfully attempting to bribe the librarian to allow me to take the reference book home with me overnight, I sat down and read avidly. This was the extraordinary story:

Anne Jefferies was born in St Teath in 1626 into an extremely poor family. As was customary at the time, once Anne was old enough to be able to perform simple household tasks, she was sent to work for a wealthy family in the neighbourhood who in return agreed to feed, clothe and give her lodgings. This family was the Pitt family, who almost certainly lived in the house now known as Tower Farm in the centre of the village.

Anne was a tom-boy, or as Moses describes her, *'a girl of a bold and daring spirit who would venture at those difficulties and dangers no boy would attempt.'* She appears to have been accepted into the Pitt household and treated almost as one of the family. However, when Anne was nineteen years old something happened which was to change Anne's life and that of those around her forever.

Anne was sitting knitting in the garden, when, as she later recounted, six small people all dressed in green came over the hedge towards her. Anne was terrified and fell into a convulsive fit. For months afterwards Anne was confined to bed, unable to walk and suffering frequent fits. She repeatedly called out, *"They are just gone out of the window! Did you not see them?"* Everyone assumed these were hallucinations due to her recurring fever. Eventually Anne recovered enough to be able to do a few simple tasks and to venture out into the garden again.

One day during the following harvest time, the Pitt household ran out of flour for the evening meal. As the servants were all working in the fields, Mrs Pitt decided to walk the short distance down to the mill herself and ask the miller to bring up more flour urgently. She did not wish to leave Anne in the house alone in case she had an accident or did something silly, so she ordered her to sit outside in the garden, which Anne did, albeit very reluctantly.

On the way home Mrs Pitt slipped and fell, injuring her leg so badly that she was unable to stand. Fortunately a neighbour on horseback came by and carried Mrs Pitt back to the house where she lay on the couch in great pain. A servant was ordered to saddle up the horse and ride to Bodmin to fetch the doctor. However, at this point, Anne came in and begged Mrs Pitt to let her see the injured leg. She took the leg on her lap and stroked it gently, saying that she was sure she could heal it. After a while a sceptical Mrs Pitt had to admit that the leg did indeed feel better. She told the servant to wait a while and a short time later instructed him to unsaddle the horse, as the doctor would not be needed. When questioned, Anne revealed that the fairies had been visiting her regularly since that first day in the garden and it was they who had caused Mrs Pitt's accident. She said they were annoyed with Mrs Pitt because she had not let Anne stay in the house as she had wanted, when Mrs Pitt went to the mill. The fairies had then explained to Anne how she could cure the injured leg, which to everyone's astonishment she proceeded to do.

The news of this miraculous cure and of the fairies' part in this healing spread rapidly throughout Cornwall and beyond. Soon people with all kinds of illnesses and injuries were flocking to St Teath from as far afield as London to be cured by Anne. *'She took no money of them nor any reward'*, writes Moses, *'She neither made nor bought any medicines or salves, yet wanted them not, as she had occasion.'*

Soon after this Anne stopped eating with the family, saying that she was being fed by the fairies. She was able to predict accurately which people would come to the house, where they would have travelled from and what time they would arrive, all this several days in advance. Anne's fame grew and became such that the local magistrates and ministers began to take an interest in this girl with the mysterious powers. They came to the Pitts' house demanding to see Anne and interrogated her thoroughly on everything that had happened. As Moses states, *'She gave them very rational answers to all their questions, the whole family affirming the truth of all she said.'* Nevertheless the magistrates declared that Anne was consorting with evil spirits and that her extraordinary powers were *'delusions of the devil.'*

The evening after this visit, Mr Pitt tried to explain the dangers of the situation to Anne and to convince her of the risks she was taking. It was a perilous time to be accused of consorting with evil spirits. Elsewhere in the country witch-hunts were at their height and scores of so-called witches were being tried, tortured and put to death by hanging. The Pitt family were only too aware of these horrific events and of the dangers Anne's behaviour could bring to them all. Mr Pitt tried to convince Anne of the gravity of the magistrates' pronouncements and to persuade her not to listen to these 'fairies' any more. For a while that evening Anne did resist the fairies' calls for her to go to them in her chamber and she reluctantly stayed downstairs by the fireside with the family However, despite Mr Pitt's dire warnings, she finally gave in and rushed upstairs to her bedroom. Shortly afterwards she returned to the family holding a Bible which she insisted the fairies had instructed her to show everyone. It was open at the *1st Epistle of St John, Chapter 4, verse 1*. A surprised Mr Pitt read out, *'Dearly beloved, believe not every spirit, but try the spirits whether they be of God.'* This was greeted with a shocked silence. Everyone knew that Anne could not read a word.

Anne continued to perform her healings as before until one fateful day John Tregeagle, the notoriously cruel JP and steward to the Earl of Radnor, sent a constable to St Teath with a warrant for Anne's arrest. Tregeagle's reputation for the particularly harsh and merciless manner in which he dealt with both defendants and tenants was well-known throughout Cornwall, Anne was apparently warned by the fairies that her arrest was about to happen, but was told not to resist since the fairies would take care of her. To the family's great consternation Anne was taken away and incarcerated in Bodmin Gaol, where her guards were ordered not to give her food or drink of any kind.

At Anne's trial in court both Mrs Pitt and the young boy, Moses were questioned under oath and accused of secretly supplying Anne with food, a charge both vehemently denied. After this, although no verdict is recorded, Anne was kept in prison and deprived of food and water for several months. When she showed no signs of ill effects on her health Tregeagle, obviously suspecting some kind of trickery, transferred her to his own house, Trevorder in the parish of Wadebridge. There she was kept under lock and key for a further three months with absolutely no means of obtaining sustenance of any kind. At the end of this time, to Tregeagle's great frustration and bewilderment, Anne appeared to be as fit and healthy as she had always been and the steward felt compelled to release her, but with the condition that she should no longer live with the Pitts in St Teath. Accordingly Mr Pitt arranged for Anne to go and live with his sister, Mrs Frances Tom, a widow, in Padstow. We have no record of Anne performing any further cures there.

Many years later in 1691, Moses, recently released from debtors' prison in London and desperately in need of cash, clearly saw the publication of this account of the strange events of his childhood as a possible means of earning some money. Moses wrote to his nephew in Cornwall asking him to try to find someone in St Teath who could verify the events in his account. When asked, both Moses' mother and his grandmother were able to confirm that Anne had indeed been imprisoned in Bodmin Gaol where she had lived for six months without food. In addition his mother said that she herself recalled seeing the fairies, but only on one occasion. Anne herself was still alive and almost seventy at this time but, when questioned, stated categorically that she could not remember anything from fifty years ago.

Moses did not give up but asked his brother-in-law, Humphrey Martyn to go to Padstow and do his best to persuade Anne to give her own version of these extraordinary events. Humphrey wrote back telling Moses he had spent most of the day with Anne and had read her Moses' account. Anne had refused to say anything at all about the events concerning the fairies or the cures she had performed., saying, *"If I should discover it to you, you would make books or ballads of it and I would not have my name spread about the country in books or ballads if I might have £500 for doing it."* Anne was obviously afraid that if the story were to be published and brought to the notice of the magistrates, she could be put on trial again. Humphrey did, however, manage to track down an old man, Thomas Christopher, a former servant in the Pitt household, who remembered many of the incidents mentioned in the account. Moses' younger sister, Mary said that, although she had been very young at the time and could not remember the events themselves, she recalled her parents telling her all about them.

It is a fascinating and puzzling story. There have, of course, been many stories of faith healings throughout history and up to the present day, so this aspect of the story is not unique. As for Anne's claim to have been fed by the fairies, it is possible that Anne had managed to find some way of obtaining food whilst in the Pitt household, but how she survived her months of imprisonment in Bodmin Gaol and, even more mysteriously, in the home of the notorious Jan Tregeagle, is more difficult - if not impossible - to explain.

What Moses does not mention, however, was the fact that Anne's arrest may have been for more than witchcraft. During the Civil War Cornwall was mainly on the side of the King, so Tregeagle and the rest of Cromwell's Parliamentarian supporters were not popular with many of the Cornish people. Letters in the Bodleian Library written in 1647, the year when Cromwell finally defeated the King's armies and took over the ruling of the country, give details of '*Ye Prophetesse of Bodmin*' and corroborate Moses' account of Anne's cures, her premonitions, her fasting and her encounters with fairies. However one of these letters also quotes Anne as saying, "*The King shall enjoy his own and berevenged of his enemies.*" Tregeagle and the Parliamentarian authorities were very wary of any remaining support for the Royalist cause at these uncertain times. It appears Anne was in prison *'lest her discourses which are all on behalf of the King and against Parliament should trouble the peoples' minds, who are apt to revolt from the Parliament's obedience.'*

After her release Anne lived in Padstow, eventually marrying a certain William Warren. There does not appear to be any record of when Anne died or where she is buried. St Teath's Parish Records do, however, give us details of Anne's parents : Philip Jefferies married Jane Hick on 18th January 1620. Baptisms of the couple's six children, two of whom died in infancy, are also recorded, although the exact day and month of Anne's baptism in the year 1626 are no longer legible. Local legend places her family's cottage as the little house now known as Primrose Cottage, very near to Tower Farm, but it could have been any of the other old cottages by the church which form the original part of the village. The Pitts' farm, where Anne lived and worked, was almost certainly the 16th century house, now known as *Tower Farm* and previously called *Pitts' Tenement.*

Although it is uncertain when Anne died, her life appears to have been a long and happy one, since she was still alive and well in 1693 aged nearly seventy, which was long-lived for those times. However, Jan Tregeagle for his part became even more notorious in Cornish legend for his evil doings and was ultimately condemned to the endless task of emptying the bottomless lake of Dozmary Pool with a leaky limpet shell. It is clear whose side the Little People were on.

Chapter Six

The Clock Tower

It was a crisp, icy-cold New Year's Eve. We were standing in the Square where other villagers, young and old, were gathering in small groups, as the hands on the clock high on St Teath's iconic Clock Tower crept towards midnight. Each of the four clock faces showed a slightly different time and when I remarked on this to one of the locals, back came his response, "Well, what would be the point in having *four* clockfaces if they all showed exactly the same time?" Suddenly, with little more than a minute to go on the clock that was way out in front, the door to the White Hart pub burst open and a crowd of revellers streamed out, many in fancy dress, shouting and laughing. Everyone quickly joined hands to form a huge circle around the clock tower, just as the chimes rang out, prompting everyone to burst into a hearty, if not altogether harmonious, rendering of *Auld Lang Syne*.

As the singing came to an end, three or four young men pointed to a very old man, sporting an unconvincing long, grey beard and brandishing a scythe, who was shuffling up the road towards the clock. Round his neck was a placard with 1975 writ large. From the opposite direction came another fellow, pushing a wheelbarrow containing a giant baby, complete with nappy and bonnet, waving merrily and bearing a sign proclaiming 1976. The young lads chased the old man out of the Square to loud applause from the crowd and the baby, who bore a striking resemblance to a local builder, was welcomed with cheers and much merriment.   Everyone went round giving hugs and wishing friends and neighbours a Happy New Year, then pulled their woolly hats down over their ears and headed for home under a sky scattered with stars.   It was a good way to start the New Year.

I noticed that Mrs Best, our neighbour's friend who was usually a great supporter of local traditions, had been missing from the New Year's Eve celebrations. There was a reason for this, as she explained days later.

"People forget this is a War Memorial," she told me, "I don't think it shows proper respect for those young men who lost their lives fighting for our freedom, when people go singing and dancing round it like that – especially as most of them have had too much to drink."

My thoughts went back to the time just after the end of World War I when the idea for St Teath's War Memorial first came about.   With the help of old newspaper reports and a trawl through the Church Logbook, I was able to piece together the following account.

It was Rev Claude Kingdon, the enterprising and resourceful curate-in-charge at St Teath during this time, who instigated the plan to build a monument in the centre of the village to honour the ten local men who had given their lives in the service of their country.   With the help of a small committee, he persuaded Oswald Swete, manager of the newly-reopened Treburgett mine, to design the clock tower and to act as Clerk of Works for the building operation, all without any financial reward. The stone needed was given free of charge by Adolphus Beer (what splendid names these people had) owner of the local quarry, and the slates for the roof were donated by Delabole Slate Co. The cost of the clock itself and other materials, £390 in total, was raised by subscription and fundraising. It was an impressive community effort and most commendable of all was the fact that village artisans, builders and stonemasons each agreed to give 48 hours' free labour to bring the project to fruition.

The foundation stone was laid on July 24th 1920 with due ceremony and a special outdoor service in the Square, conducted by the vicar Rev Edwardes and attended by many villagers.

The completed memorial was unveiled five months later on Dec 18th at a commemoration service attended by local dignitaries and the whole village. After hymns and prayers, Mrs J Williams, wife of the Lord-Lieutenant of Cornwall released the large Union Jack which had covered the front of the monument and revealed the plaque with the names of those who had died. The ten names poignantly include three pairs of brothers. Mrs Williams, who had herself lost two sons in the war, gave a moving address, expressing the hope that the memorial would stand to ensure that future generations would never forget the sacrifice made by these men. Two buglers from the DCLI sounded the Last Post and relatives of the dead laid wreathes at the foot of the tower. Rev Kingdon must have felt justly proud of such a splendid achievement.

The newspaper report lavishes praise on the members of such a small community for raising this impressive monument and for *'the unity which led to the consummation of the work.'* However, as a reminder that those noble villagers were nevertheless only human, I should add that the unity did not last much beyond the unveiling ceremony. A stone plaque over the door to the tower originally bore the names of the committee and builders involved, but a bitter dispute over whose names should have been included resulted in the plaque having to be reworked. No agreement could be reached, so the names were eventually erased completely and the blank stone plaque still stands over the door today. However, more importantly, St Teath's beautiful Clock Tower itself also still stands. as was intended, as a lasting memorial to the sacrifice made by those gallant young men.

The newly-built War Memorial 1920

Chapter Seven

Treburgett Mine

In the Spring following our move to Cornwall, we decided to try to tame a small area of the wilderness which had once been a back garden, to allow us to grow vegetables. I was digging a trench for the potatoes when a voice came from the other side of the hedge:

"I wouldn't dig too deep, if I were you."

I went to the gate to behold a young man, in proper hiker's gear of boots, tracksuit and cagoule striding past up the hill.

"Why not?" I called out, thinking he was about to give me some much-needed advice on the cultivation of vegetables.

He pointed to a spot on the map which hung in a plastic holder around his neck, "Well, according to this map there's a mine under here, " he informed me in an authoritative tone.

The ruined engine house of Treburgett Mine was still standing at this time as a landmark on the horizon at the top of the field opposite our cottage. Henry Lyle, the village butcher, and his sister, Glenice had told me how, as children, they had lived in Treburgett and how they and all the children from the hamlet used to play in the old ruins of the mine. The boys enjoyed sliding down the waste-dumps on bits of corrugated tin. In the winter when the water from the tank on a high wall had been dripping all night and frozen, they would fight with 6ft long icicles. The girls played 'house' in the ruined engine house, making 'fuzzy cakes' - mud-pies decorated with furze-bush flowers. However, the fact that the mine workings could have extended as far as our cottage was news to me. This was a potentially alarming discovery, as I pictured returning from the shops one day to find our home had collapsed into a disused mineshaft. More visits to the reference library were definitely needed.

In a volume entitled *Mines and Miners of Cornwall* by A.K. Hamilton Jenkins I found meticulously detailed descriptions of every mine in Cornwall, including all the workings in and around St Teath, at Trewennan, Pengenna, Treroosel, Treburgett and, sure enough, Whitewell. The history of the mine is a fascinating one, going back to the beginning of the 1800s. At this time a German miner is said to have discovered, *'to great rejoicing in the neighbourhood with firing of guns and hoisting of flags'* a lead-antimony lode (antimony is a silver-grey metal used as an alloy to strengthen lead) probably in the region of Pengenna. Shortly after this, the finding of a lode of lead ore close to the surface resulted in the starting up of Treburgett Mine, managed by Nicholas Ennor, a miner of considerable repute throughout the county.

Nicholas Ennor lived at Ennormead, the house now known as Trevellan on the hill leading into St Teath from Knights Mill. His imposing stone tomb with its ornate decoration and Latin inscription is perched almost on top of the hedge by the main entrance into the churchyard opposite the Church Hall. He was in charge of Treburgett Mine from 1817 - 1826, when the mine was worked extensively and described as having the richest lead lode in the whole of Cornwall. However when the mine reached a depth of around 360ft, its small pumping engine was no longer capable of dealing with the surge of water and the mine was drowned out.

For over thirty years the mine remained idle, although various lodes were explored and eventually abandoned by prospectors at Trewennan, Treroosal and Lower Suffenton. During this time the waste from Treburgett mine workings had been used by local farmers for repairing walls and hedges. One auspicious day a mineralogist on a visit to St Teath and out walking around the fields made the momentous discovery that this waste in fact contained pure silver. As a result of this in 1869 a new company was formed with the aim of producing both silver and lead and Treburgett mine reopened with a larger, more powerful pump engine. The mine worked very successfully for the next ten years, employing around 200 men, women and children and producing large amounts of both silver and lead.

Tributing, the traditional method of mining, was still current at this time. Each man was virtually self-employed and miners would bid against each other for a particular working area, after which it was up to each man's own skill and hard work to determine how much he earned. The workers would walk to Treburgett across the fields and then climb down slippery wooden ladders to the work face. It was a dangerous job and accidents were not uncommon. A gravestone in St Teath cemetery bears witness to the death of Joseph Bickle, a young boy aged just 13 when in January 1874 he was killed in the mine.

Despite these years of prosperity, in 1880 Treburgett Mine was yet again forced to close, this time due to disputes regarding finances and the falling price of lead. Once again the mine remained idle for decades until in 1919, after the end of World War I, Treburgett Consolidated Mines Ltd started up under the management of Oswald Swete. The opening was announced with great excitement and optimism in all the local newspapers. About 45 staff, nearly all ex-servicemen, were employed and a great deal of work was done in preparing the mine for the new venture. The old mine stack was demolished, new buildings constructed and the road to the site renewed. It was expected that the initial output would be in the region of 250 tons of ore per week, rising to 500 tons over time. The ore would be taken to nearby Port Isaac Road Station, whence it would be transported to Padstow by rail and onward by ship to Swansea for smelting.

Unfortunately it seems these great hopes were never realised, as there are no records of any ore being produced at Treburgett at this time. Nor are there any more reports of further activity at the mine – until years later Henry, Glenice and their young friends transformed it into their adventure playground. Today you can still walk across the fields on the path the miners would have taken, but all that remains of the once-thriving mine is a ruined chimney stack and a few broken walls, overgrown with trees and gorse, and instead of the clamour of men and machines there is total silence and the occasional song of a lone blackbird.

Chapter Eight

A charismatic curate

As I became immersed in the past life of the village, I began to feel as if I knew some of its former residents almost as well as those living here today. It was while researching the origins of the Clock Tower that I made the acquaintance of the character who was to become one of my favourites: the Rev Claude Kingdon.

Rev Kingdon, nephew of Rev Hawker, the renowned Vicar of Morwenstow, came to St Teath in 1917 as curate-in-charge and threw himself wholeheartedly into his calling from the very beginning. The war was still going on, but he organised social events and entertainments of all kinds to lift people's spirits. In that first summer the vicarage lawn became the venue for all kinds of fund-raising activities, fun sports and afternoon teas. *'Come and be happy!'* Rev KIngdon's hand-written posters said, *'And make others happy!'* In the winter that followed the enterprising vicar put on concerts in which villagers displayed their talents for music and recitation and Rev Kingdon himself was, according to the local newspaper, *'the star turn of the evening'* singing comic songs and telling jokes. He was then joined by the equally game Mrs Kingdon and their duets reportedly *'brought the house down.'* Proceeds went to the Red Cross. The next summer he arranged outings to Polzeath and

Widemouth Bay for over a hundred members of the choir and Church Catechism group to enjoy days at the seaside.

A theatre group, the St Teath Pierrots, was formed and funds were raised to provide parcels for our 'boys at war'.

.

At a Village Fete the following year an incredible 1,100 people were recorded as passing through the vicarage gates, including twenty-five American soldiers from Bowithick Camp who together with the hundred fete helpers were all given a free tea. There was a cricket match between St Teath Ladies and the Sidesmen (whose team members could only bat and bowl left-handedly). This was won by the Ladies, 49 runs to 34. Camelford Town Band played, there was Maypole Dancing and stalls and games galore. The day was rounded off by an al fresco concert and a parade through the village, followed by Evensong in a packed church. Little did Rev Kingdon know that his custom of holding a Fete of this kind on the vicarage lawn to celebrate St Tetha's Dedication Day on Whit Monday, was to continue for over sixty years. right up until the time when the vicarage itself was sold and the vicar housed in a smaller, modern house.

A newspaper report of the evening concert paints a vivid portrait of the man: *'Rev C.D. Kingdon was just himself and those who know him and have heard him will need no further comment. Mr Kingdon is one of those men who could run a concert on his own if the necessity arose, for he is a veritable host all by himself. His songs and stories provided just the mental tonic and the opportunity to laugh that is so badly needed in these days when we are at war in the grimmest sense of the term'.*

Rev Kingdon was deeply moved by the deaths on active service of so many young men from the village, as his sensitive recording of each family's bereavement in the

Church log shows. By November 1917 he had raised funds for the erection of a War Shrine in the churchyard with a crucifix and the names of those from the parish who had fallen in the war. The following year he formed a committee to oversee the erection in the Square of a monument inscribed with these young men's names, surmounted by a clock. The story of this memorial's creation has already been told.

Not satisfied with having set this major construction plan in motion, later that same year Rev Kingdon declared his intention to carry out an ambitious plan to build a Church Hall *'with dressing rooms, copper, fittings and chairs suitable for teas, concerts, lantern lectures etc'* Such a building was certainly needed, as until now all social gatherings, including parties for over a hundred people where games and dancing took place, all happened in the small Church Room (the present Community Centre) with larger gatherings and concerts being held in the village school – or on the Vicarage lawn. His plan was to purchase the Bible Christian Chapel, (on the site subsequently taken by St Teath Garage and now the Koth Karji development) and extend it to the size needed for a Church Hall. He bought the Chapel, using his own money, but was not allowed to buy the land next to it, so a change of plan became necessary. Originally he had thought to build on a plot of glebe land to the south of the church, so he now bought that plot too, again with money from his own pocket. He demolished the Bible Christian Chapel to enable the stone, wood and slate to be used as building materials for the new Church Hall. The total cost of land and Chapel was £200.

From now on fundraising events would be directed solely towards the building of a Church Hall.. The Whitsun Village Fete that year included an Auction, the poster for which, in Rev Kingdon's inimitable style, reads: *Kind gifts are asked for the Sale: Ducks, chickens, rabbits (dead or alive), potatoes, pigs, furniture, china, glass, toys, ornaments, silver, pictures, pea-sticks, bicycles, vegetables, books, novels, puppies, jewellery, watches, carpets, cats, kittens, plants, eggs, chairs, pottery, tools, lamps, candlesticks, games, bags, boats, pipes, curtains, razors, rugs, gloves, jam, music, cutlery, fenders, cakes, ferrets, pigeons, opera-glasses, fishing rods, walking sticks, guns, cheques. Proceeds to the new Church Hall. Don't use this circular for lighting your pipe or curling your hair! Kindly send something for the sale – and come and be an enthusiastic bidder or send someone with your purse!*

The amazing sum of £100 was raised in one afternoon. When you consider that you could buy a small cottage for this price at that time, it shows the enormity of the achievement. Rev Kingdon was encouraged to pursue his plan of borrowing money to enable building work on the Hall to start as soon as possible. In the meantime fundraising was going on apace with the next year's Fete raising an even more astounding £135.

Enterprising and enthusiastic as he was about these events and schemes, it is clear that Rev Kingdon did not neglect to put his calling as parish priest above all other considerations. His letters to his parishioners are full of exhortations for them to attend church services and take communion regularly with due reverence and devotion. Indeed, he must have been an inspiring and engaging preacher, as the church was always packed for his services and over a hundred communicants regularly took part. He was called on to speak at an important Priests' Convention in Cambridge in 1922 to *'set out the truths of our Holy Catholic Faith with no uncertain voice'* and defend it against 'modernist' attacks. One can imagine that he would have proved a forceful and highly effective speaker.

In February of 1923 Rev Kingdon announced that a tender had been accepted from a consortium of four local builders and work had commenced on building the Hall. The tender was for £1,066 and fundraising events so far had brought in £310. His plea to all parishioners was for donations or subscriptions to clear the debt of £756 by the proposed completion date of May 1st. He proposed a scheme whereby subscribers could give a basic amount immediately with a promise of further subscriptions in the future, thus enabling him to pay the contractors on completion. He himself generously set the ball rolling by giving a first subscription of £100 with a promise of a further £100 for the next two years, thereby reducing the sum needed now to £456 - with the hope of raising a further £106 at that year's Fete when it was planned to have the official opening ceremony.

Shortly after this, Rev Kingdon made the surprise announcement that *'following the stern path of duty'* he would be making an *'undesired but necessary'* move in the coming summer to the Rectory of Whitstone in Devon. This led to increasingly frantic pleas for donations, as he himself had guaranteed to pay off the remaining debt to the contractors by Opening Day. His intention had been to borrow the money in the expectation that this amount could easily be raised by concerts and other events once the new Hall was up and running. His imminent departure from St Teath now meant that he was personally responsible for this debt. He wrote ever more desperately to villagers:

'The walls are rapidly rising and I do not wish to leave a legacy of debt on this building, so, although this will cripple me for the next three years, I have reduced the cost to £356 and this debt, unless cleared by my appeal, will fall on me, my heirs and assigns and so I do ask those who wish a share in this building, to contribute AT ONCE.'

With two subscriptions of £5 and promises of a further £5 the next year, he was not exactly overwhelmed by the response from villagers.

The date of the Opening was set for May 16th, the Wednesday before the Village Fete. The ceremony was conducted by the Archdeacon of Bodmin who led a service of dedication and a rather appropriate Battle Hymn was sung. The Vicar, Rev Edwardes, resident in Delabole, said how grateful he had been for Rev Kingdon's help over the years and that the Hall could never have been built without his generosity. Rev Kingdon proposed a vote of thanks to the architect and contractors and said his contribution to the project had been *'a thanks offering to God for sparing him his life after five serious operations and for the six happy years He had allowed him to spend in St Teath'*. The poor man then made a last desperate appeal for the £200 still needed to clear the debt.

That evening a concert in the new Hall brought in over £36 and the Village Fete a few days later raised nearly £100. There is therefore every hope that by the end of June, when Rev and Mrs Kingdon sat in the comfortable armchairs, presented to them by the village, and enjoyed a farewell tea and entertainment, the debt on the Hall may have finally been cleared. It must nevertheless have been with a mixture of regret and relief that this extraordinary man bade farewell to St Teath.

Chapter Nine

Chapels

The Church Log tells us that as a first step in the building of the Church Hall, Rev Kingdon had bought up the disused Bible Christian Chapel. I was aware of the two large Methodist chapels on Trevilley Lane but this third one was news to me. However I was soon to learn that there was in fact an astonishing total of *nine* chapels in the area: one in Trewalder, three in Delabole, one in Treligga, one in Trelill and the three in St Teath, all built during the great surge of Methodism which swept the county following John Wesley's visits at the end of the 18th century.

Wesley visited Cornwall over 40 times between 1743 and 1780 and had a great influence on church-going especially among the miners, quarrymen and the poor. He often came to Camelford and Trewalder where he stayed at the home of Christopher and Joan Male. Those first few years were a difficult time to be holding meetings, as it was a time of great political tension. There were fears of a French invasion and rumours that Bonnie Prince Charlie, the Young Pretender had landed in Cornwall, where many families were sympathetic to the old king's cause and the old Catholic religion. Any large gatherings were regarded with suspicion and in the early days Wesley's meetings were often broken up and people arrested.

Wesley travelled on horseback and the journey was often gruelling, with the Cornish climate only making it worse. A glance through his diary entries for his *summer* visits to this area show what he was up against:

August 1750: I preached at St Gennys at noon but with little effect. Thence we hastened to Camelford where I preached in the main street, the rain pouring down all the time but that neither drove the congregation away nor hindered the blessing of God. The next day I preached at Trewalder. Many were dissolved into gracious tears and many filled with strong consolation.

August 1751: I rode to Port Isaac and thence to Trewalder. The little society here meet every night and morn with a preacher or without and whoever comes among them quickly feels what spirit they are of. The next day the rain stopped at noon and gave me the opportunity of preaching in the marketplace at Camelford. I saw only one person who was not deeply moved. That one I am sorry to say was the curate of the parish. As soon as we set out to ride onwards we were met with such a downpour of rain as I never saw before in Europe.

August 1757: We rode through vehement wind and many hard showers to Camelford. This gave me a violent fit of toothache which however did not hinder my preaching. The next day I preached at Trewalder and found God was there. In the evening, the rain having become intermittent,

I preached in Camelford marketplace now one of the liveliest places in Cornwall.
August 1776: *I was going to preach in the marketplace at Camelford when a violent storm drove us into the house...*

Wesley died in 1791, but the dynamism of the Methodist movement continued to grow with a formidable number of societies springing up all over the country many of which still exist today. In Cornwall particularly there followed a huge drive to build chapels in every neighbourhood, often reflecting the different branches of Methodism. In 1810 William O'Bryan, a local Wesleyan preacher broke away from the main Methodists in North Cornwall and founded the branch known as the Bible Christians. This was a more democratic form of Methodism with no hierarchy. From its humble beginnings in Cornwall and Devon, it grew to become a nationwide movement, though its custom of allowing ordinary lay people, including women, to preach sermons, often outdoors, was scorned by many Anglicans. *"The inhabitants amuse themselves on Sundays by having one or other of those fatuous enthusiasts, the Bryanites, to preach, or more properly to rave nonsense,"* comments one contemporary local historian, Frederick Trevan.

St Teath's Bible Christian Chapel was built in 1833, on the site subsequently occupied by the garage and currently by the Koth Karji housing development. O'Bryan himself preached in St Teath many times. A local wrestling champion from Treligga, Abraham Bastard (with the accent on the second syllable) - *'a man feared in every arena from the Tamar to the Lizard'* - became a convert and acted as bouncer at these meetings. On one such occasion, a woman preacher, Betsy Reed was addressing the congregation but was constantly interrupted by the local blacksmith. Abraham warned him to be quiet but when he continued to heckle, Abraham seized hold of him, *"Do 'ee think God's people are to be interrupted in any way by the devil's servants?"* he demanded and attempted to remove the heckler from the chapel. However the blacksmith clung to the door and would not let go, whereupon Abraham dislodged both blacksmith and door and removed both from the building.

The chapel, originally accommodating 150 people found its congregation diminishing with the opening of the two much larger United Methodist Chapels in Trevilley Lane in 1869 and by the end of the century had fallen into disuse, until Rev Kingdon found a purpose for it as building material for the new Church Hall. The Sunday School on Trevilley Lane was converted into an art studio in the 1980s and is now a private house. The St Teath Methodist Chapel held its final service in 2019, bringing to a close the 200 year reign of non-conformist religion in the village.

Wedding at the Chapel in the 1920s

Chapter Ten

The Village School

When, during that first year of our move to Cornwall, I waited each afternoon at the gate with the other mums collecting their children from school, I felt sorry for the teachers who, although living in such a beautiful part of the world, were unable to enjoy it to the full, as they had to spend so much time cooped up in a stuffy classroom. As the years went by I became aware of the extraordinarily relaxed, happy atmosphere of the village school and the open, friendly relationship between staff and pupils and a tinge of envy crept in. I began to regret no longer being part of the educational community.

My last teaching post before leaving London had been as a lecturer in English as a Second Language. I had started my teaching career in Birmingham teaching French in a boys' grammar school and I had also worked in a Primary school in West London. Astonishing as it may seem nowadays, at that time before PGCE certificates and B.Ed degrees, it was assumed that if you had a degree, you could teach anyone anything. However, it seemed to me that the chances of finding employment as a teacher of English as a Second language in Cornwall, when I had not seen a single person of any minority ethnic background since arriving here, were rather slim.

However, when Mr Crosley, Head of St Teath School at that time suggested I might like to register with County as a Supply Teacher, to enable him to call on me to cover for absent teachers when necessary, I readily agreed. I did not want a fulltime job as Tasha was only a toddler and there was still much work needed to make the cottage habitable, but an occasional spell of teaching in the village school and other schools in the local area seemed ideal.

My first day as a teacher in St Teath school was a revelation. The children were polite and well-behaved, but very eager to chat away telling me all about their families and their lives outside school. The conversation was natural and open. When playtime came, I was surprised to find that the teachers stood around in the hall to drink tea and talk. When I asked where the staffroom was, I was told there wasn't one. "We don't need one," I was told. Children wandered in and out at will, sometimes talking to the staff or sometimes just sitting on the floor reading books, but it was true we had no need of a refuge away from these children. The Head's 'Office' was a corner of his classroom, with a desk, a chair and a telephone – and a pile of dirty dishes from the previous day's lunch. The whole atmosphere was totally different from the schools where I had worked in cities. This was, of course, due mainly to the small number of children in the school, then around seventy pupils, in comparison with the hundreds in Birmingham and London.

When I joined the school in the 1970s, Mr Crosley had already been Head teacher for over twenty years and knew the children and their families almost as well as his own. He continued as Head until 1980 – a tenure of 27 years. He was not alone in this long service record as Mr William Parsons who retired in 1930 had also served as Head for 27 years. However the Infant Teacher, Mrs Kyle Burden retired in 1972 having taught in St Teath school for an unassailable record of 42 years, only to continue coming into school on a voluntary basis to play the piano for many years more. Mr Graham Dunn, the Head following Mr Crosley, taught here for 26 years before retiring. There was clearly something special about this place that kept people here for so long. It could not simply be the lack of public transport to get away – or the extremely warm welcome of the White Hart pub.

When tracing the history of education in the village the first mention I could find was by the historian, Sir John Maclean in 1823, when he says: '*In the village in a large room, part of the old workhouse (*the present Community Centre) *a school is kept in which about sixty of the sons of farmers etc are educated: there are various Dame Schools within the parish, in which instruction is afforded to about 180 other children; 108 are educated in a British and Foreign School at Pengelly, which is under government inspection. In addition to the daily schools abovementioned, a Sunday School is held in the Church and also in some of the Dissenters' Meeting Houses which are attended by about 120 children.'*. There was a Dame School, a small private school presided over by a Schoolmistress, in Trewennan Manor and another in the cottage opposite the White Hart, but where the many others were is unknown.

In the Census of 1841 John Oliver gives his occupation as Schoolmaster and a memorial in the churchyard states that he was Schoolmaster for 59 years. A census twenty years later also describes Nathaniel Hawken as Schoolmaster, but there is no indication as to where in the village either of these men taught. Children would travel in from outlying areas, sometimes as far away as Blisland, boarding with families in St Teath during the week and going home at weekends.

In 1875 the St Teath School Board was set up to provide Elementary Education for children aged 3 to 12 in the parish and to build new schools for this purpose in Delabole and St Teath. The first site to be considered was the field behind Union Row, but eventually the present site, then known as Homer New Parks, was purchased from a Mr Philp for £2. Mr Sylvanus Trevail, a well-known architect of the time, was engaged to design the schools. Delabole School was designed to house 340 boys and girls (taught separately) and St Teath 165 children (mixed classes). The plans went out to tender and Mr John Oliver was given the contract with £4,800 for both schools.

The Board advertised for a Master and a Mistress, the latter just to teach sewing. The proviso, *'Teetotallers preferred'* was added, showing the strong Methodist influence on the board of the time. St Teath School finally opened on 9th December 1878 with Mr Frank Down as Master and his wife, Emily as Assistant Teacher. In addition there were two Monitors or Pupil-Teachers – pupils who stayed on past the school leaving age to work as apprentice teachers. Twenty-five children were admitted on that first day. The Board gave each school an annual grant to cover all running expenses, including the pay of teachers and any other staff. This was dependent on high pupil attendance and good exam results. Members of the Board visited the school regularly without notice to check registers, discipline and standards of teaching. Mr Down received his first Board visit only a week after opening, when numbers of pupils had already doubled, but the new Master was not impressed by their academic skills, as he commented in the School Log, *'The children are very ignorant ; out of the whole on the books (49) only four can say the multiplication table.'*

At the start of the new term after Christmas, numbers of children doubled once more and continued to increase until by July there were 168 children attending the school, still with only Mr and Mrs Down plus two Pupil-Teachers on the staff It was not until a year later in January 1880 that a second Assistant teacher, Mr Bennet was appointed. This teacher's career ended abruptly in shame and ignominy after only one year, due to his attempt to conduct a secret affair with a Pupil-Teacher, employing pupils to convey love letters between classrooms. Mr Down's discovery of this dastardly affair is described in forensic detail in the school's Log Book.

Throughout the year Mr Down repeatedly complains about the Pupil-Teacher, Mary Ellen Ellery, who is regularly late and has never prepared her lessons. The Head then notices that whenever the teacher, Mr Bennet enters the room Mary Ellen blushes. *'So, of course, I tried by various means to discover the root of this mischief but failed until this afternoon. I altered the timetable, giving Mr Bennet the 2nd Standard Arithmetic cards in a bag to be used by his class in the first lesson and told Mary Ellen to use the same cards in her class for the second lesson. The time to change lessons came and the cards had to be taken from Mr Bennet's class to Mary Ellen's room. In transit I took the bag from the boy's hand and opened it and saw a love letter written by Mr Bennet.'* Mr Down then copies word-for-word the letter where Mr Bennet arranges a rendezvous with Mary-Ellen that evening. *'Out came Mr Bennet in a passion, "I will have that note, Mr Down," he said. "No, you will not." I replied. "I don't call it a manly trick of you to look in the bag," he said. "That is exactly my duty – to look in the bag and see that things are all right," I said "Well, I look and I see the note. It is plain that if you are writing such nonsense as this you cannot be doing your duty and I do not want anyone here who will not do his duty."* There follows a further account of Mr Down's detective work in tracking down the two lovebirds and the result is that the School Board gives Mr Bennet three months' notice of dismissal.

For the first two years of the school's existence children were charged fees to attend and these varied according to the parents' job: the children of a) paupers paid 1/4d (a farthing) per attendance; b) labourers, miners

& quarrymen 2d (two-pence) a week; c)tradespeople 3d a week and d) farmers 4d a week. It was not long before Mr Down had a full-scale revolt on his hands, with various tradespeople refusing to pay more than 2d a week and soon after several farmers joined in also demanding to pay 2d a week. By May the Board had sensibly relented and were charging a uniform 2d for all children, except paupers who were paid for by the Guardians of the Parish Poor. This continued until the Free Education Act was passed in 1880, when school fees were abolished.

The school year at this time started on 1st July and the longest holiday was Harvest Holiday starting in late August and lasting for three weeks, but for many children this was no holiday since they had to work long hours in the fields. The Christmas Holiday was usually two weeks but was extended if the weather was bad or if the school's supply of coal ran out. The only other holidays were one day for Good Friday and one week for Whitsuntide in early June. However, the fact that the Board's grant – and therefore the Master's stipend – was dependent on high attendance caused problems from the very start. Many parents did not share the Master's insistence on the importance of school attendance and local events often took precedence. In that first year alone the Logbook records the school had very small attendance or had to close due to: Camelford Fair, a Sunday School trip to Polzeath, another trip to Trebarwith, the Festival of the Band of Hope, the Bible Christians' Lunch, Bazaar & Tea, a circus in Camelford, a concert in aid of St Teath Poultry

Show, wild beasts(!) at Knights Mill, a Baby Show at St Tudy, the Cattle Market at Delabole and the re-opening of St Teath Parish Church after its restoration.

More worrying reasons for closing the school were outbreaks of illnesses such as measles, mumps and whooping cough, scarlet fever and influenza. In 1884 a serious outbreak of diphtheria, when one pupil died and several others fell dangerously ill, caused the school to close for ten whole weeks, during which five villagers died of the disease.

The following winter Mrs Down was reported ill, prompting this angry tirade in the Log Book from her husband: '***4th December:*** *This week Mrs Down has been absent in consequence of an illness owing, the doctor says, to the very wet state of the school house which in his opinion is unfit for human habitation. I have been obliged to disregard the timetable.* Then he writes: '***17th Dec***: *Mrs Down resumed work this week though still very weak. The school house is in a most disgraceful state and is a standing monument to....*' At this point words fail him. The next entry is a week later and says simply: '*I finish work as Master and Mrs Down finishes work as Assistant in this school.*' As if to prove the point, the ink here appears to have been smudged by damp – or tears? Mr Down had persevered as Master of St Teath school for seven years.

The new Master, Mr Henry Thomas, took charge of the school in January 1886 with a rod of iron. His wife taught needlework and his daughter, Jessie, was a Monitor. From Day One attendance figures were the

Master's over-riding concern, leading to the following scarcely believable series of entries in the summer of that year. In June Mr Thomas reported that his wife was ill: '**27th June**: *Attendance not so good. Mrs Thomas' illness is typhoid fever – from bad drainage arrangements, the doctor says.* **28th June**: *Mr May, member of the Board called with reference to Mrs Thomas's illness and suggested closing the school.*' Mr Thomas ignored this wise advice and the next day wrote this: '**29th June**: *Only 57 present – the news of Mrs Thomas's illness having spread through the neighbourhood*.' Still he persisted in opening the school, despite the obvious dangers to pupils' health. Then comes this brief entry: '**1st July**: *Numbers down to 24'*. Finally and shockingly on the next day comes this entry: '**2nd July** *On account of Mrs Thomas's death, there is no school this afternoon'*. The school was closed for one week.

Undeterred, Mr Thomas battled on obsessively, sending Attendance Officers out to round up absentees and in June of the next year triumphantly announces the highest average attendance figures ever recorded for a whole year - 81.9. In June 1889 this had risen again to over a hundred, due no doubt to Mr Thomas's tough regime. He complained bitterly that some children did not attend when there were storms of wind and rain, making no allowance for the fact that many had to walk distances of up to 3 miles He was very dismissive of other parents who did not send their children to school at 5 years old, but waited until they were 6 or 7, having no sympathy for the fact that they had to walk in from outlying farms often in the dark in the winter months. His unstinting efforts were rewarded in 1890 with an increase in the annual school grant from the Board for 'Good Merit'. Mr Thomas continued his reign as Master at St Teath for a further thirteen years before handing over to Mr William Parsons.

Momentous events such as the two World Wars seem to have made little impact on St Teath School's routine. Mr Parsons steered the school through the Great War making only occasional reference to the situation. His only comment in 1914, for instance, is to say that modifications had to be made to the timetable due to the Assistant teacher being called up for active service. Then there is virtually no mention of the war until May 1916 when he writes: *'Received a poster from County requesting children to help in the Harvest fields and a communication regarding the best use of blackberries to supplement diet in wartime.'* Then tragically in Sept 1918 he records:– *'Head leaving early to act as bearer for the funeral of one of our old boys, Gordon Amy who died of dysentery after seeing service in France.'* And finally in typically understated fashion on 11th November he announces: *' News of signing of Armistice with Germany and cessation of hostilities greeted by cheers from the children who went off at 10 to 12 to tell their parents* (A whole ten minutes early!) *Afternoon session: usual order of lessons departed from as children too excited to do much work.'* This was clearly a source of surprise and annoyance to him.

Empire Day, the following May Mr Parsons abandoned the timetable to devote the morning to *'matters Imperial. Tried to explain the difference between Patriotism and Jingoism. A nation's greatness is not a matter of square miles but of usefulness. Attendance very disappointing. Band of Hope festivals, stone-picking in the fields, measles, impetigo and ringworm are apparently in conspiracy against us.'*

Seismic events continued to have little effect on the regular school routine during World War II when Mr William Liddicoat was Head. In April 1939, the year war broke out, he reports only this: *'Received circular about tilling vegetables in Wartime.'* And in Sept that year: *'Work interrupted by session on fitting of gas masks.'* Over the next two or three years about a hundred evacuees plus two of their teachers were admitted to the school from London, Epsom and Plymouth, but Mr Liddicoat simply records their numbers and where they are from. There is no indication that this influx of such large numbers of extra children into the school caused any accommodation problems – or any disruption to the timetable. There is however this intriguing entry: *'Gas van arrived at 9.45 and about 50 children passed through it. All masks appear to have been efficient.'* One wonders what would have happened to the children wearing masks that were not efficient? Finally comes the announcement in 'May 1945 *News of Germany's complete surrender. School closed to celebrate.'*

When I joined the school in the seventies, there were still outdoor lavatories in the playground for the children and the Infant class was housed in an Elliott classroom, a Portacabin which was freezing in the winter and a hothouse in the summer. When numbers increased, the Hall had to be used as a permanent classroom, as well as serving as a library, gym and dining hall. Despite repeated applications to County for funding to provide a much-needed extension to the building, all we were given was a small portable cabin, from which the lavatories had to be removed before it could be put to use as a staffroom and Head's office. It was not until 2005, a year before his retirement, that Mr Dunn finally achieved his goal and the present building with its airy, well-appointed classrooms and offices finally came into being, and St Teath School moved into the modern age.

Centenary with Mr Crosley 1978 - in front of lavatories

Chapter Eleven

The Local History Society

Over the years I became aware that I was not alone in my interest in the village's past and my eagerness to find out more about all aspects of its history. In the 1980s several of us got together to investigate the possibility of forming a Local History Society. We put out a few feelers to see what support there would be and were overwhelmed by the numbers of villagers keen to join.

However, since we were all enthusiastic amateurs without a single 'proper' historian between us, that is anyone with a history qualification above O Level, it seemed wise to enlist the help of someone suitably qualified who would be able to guide us. That someone turned out to be the eminently knowledgeable and inspiring Mrs Veronica Chesher from Exeter University. This wonderful lady agreed to come to St Teath every Tuesday evening to lead a course in *Exploring Local History*. For three terms a packed school hall listened intently to Mrs Chesher's talks which soon became the highlight of our week. Mrs Chesher introduced us to Muster Records, Hearth Tax Returns, Churchwardens' accounts, Glebe Terriers, Tythe Maps & registers, Probate documents, wills, Kelly's Directories and all manner of treasure troves of facts and revelations about local history. Through these documents we were able to track the growth and development of the village, its buildings and its people through the ages.

Starting with that first written record of land and owners, *The Domesday Book,* compiled on the orders of William the Conqueror in 1086, we were able to identify the parish's oldest manors. The two earliest mentions are of *Polroad* and *Tremarustel*. *Polroad*, the present-day *Polrode Mill* in the Allen Valley, was held by Robert, Count of Mortain. He was William's half-brother, who had been given most of the land of Cornwall and eventually made Earl of Cornwall, in return for his support during the invasion of England. Most of today's Duchy land dates back to that held by the Earl. *Polroad* consisted of land for 3 ploughs, 3 acres of woodland and 17 acres of pasture. It supported 4 villagers, 3 small holders and a slave. Today it is a thriving Bed & Breakfast, I do not know how many people it supports but, as far as I know, it no longer has a slave. *Tremarustel*, the present *Treroosal Farm*, was held by Wihomarch and had land for one plough, one acre of meadow and one acre of woodland, supporting one smallholder and two slaves. Before 1066, it was held by Edmer showing that the present farmstead's origins go back an almost unimaginably long way.

About a hundred years later a further six manors were added to the register: *Trebidoc* (Treburgett), *Trenkioh* (Trekee), *Serfonten* (Higher Suffenton), *Surfonten* again (Lower Suffenton), *Duunaunt* (Dannonchapel) and *Bodwen*. All these names were familiar to us, since these ancient farms are still in existence today - with the exception of *Bodwen*. We examined old maps and discovered that *Bodwen* had been clearly marked on all the old maps up to the Ordinance Survey map of 1813 but had then disappeared, never to be seen again. It appeared to have been situated on land near *Higher Suffenton* farm, just above our cottage. Our curiosity was aroused and a small group of us asked Mr Dunston, the farmer, for permission to search his fields for any remains of this mysterious manor.

Norden's map of 1610 showing Bedwene (Bodwyn)

We spent a very pleasant, but ultimately fruitless, summer afternoon tramping over farmland and poking about in the undergrowth, convinced that we would find at the very least some pieces of masonry to show where this manor house had been, but we found nothing.

Reluctant to give up, I consulted Mrs Chesher who suggested that aerial photos sometimes show up unsuspected historical settlements. My husband used to fly a small light aircraft from Cardinham airfield at that time, so I persuaded him to fly over these same fields and take photographs that might reveal some sign of where this elusive manor could have been. Again there was nothing. It was a mystery.

Months later when looking through Hitchins & Drew's *History of Cornwall* (1824), I discovered the following: *'Bodwen, which was an ancient seat of the Nicholls family and which was afterwards purchased by the Cheneys, has been wholly demolished.'* At last we had conclusive evidence of what had happened to our lost manor, even if we did not know why. There are records of Squire Cheney owning large areas of land and many properties around St Teath in the reign of Edward III (1357). Legend has it that he was a cruel landlord whose main occupation was hunting with hounds. It is said that in rough and stormy weather, the baying of Cheney's hounds can be heard anywhere from Cheney Downs (now *China Downs* on the Delabole road) to *Trewornan Bridge* on the outskirts of Wadebridge.

Glimpses of life in mediaeval times can be seen in the personal journals of a few local gentry and in the Assession Rolls of the various parts of the county. For instance we know that a certain John Trehannick, yeoman, whose family had owned Trehannick Mill from the early 1300s, joined the ranks of the rebels supporting Perkin

Warbeck in the uprising of 1497. Warbeck, who claimed to be Richard IV, one of the Princes in the Tower, had already tried twice without success to lead an army to depose Henry VII. He now landed near Land's End to make a third attempt and marched up through Cornwall gathering hundreds of supporters as he went. Henry VII sent summons to all Cornish nobles and gentry to assemble their men and show their support for the king, but many lesser gentry who were already unhappy with the way Henry had treated them, joined the rebellion. By the time Warbeck reached Bodmin he had an army of 3,000 men and John Trehannick went to swell their ranks. What happened to him when Warbeck and his band of 6,000 men surrendered to the king's army at Blackheath a few months later was unknown to me – until very recently. As I was reading through the Family History section of *Gilbert's Survey of Cornwall,* I discovered that, although he did not accompany the insurgents to Blackheath, John did nevertheless *'continue riotously in arms.'* For this he was 'attainted' by Henry in 1503, this meant that he was stripped of his nobility, his land and his income and his heirs would no longer be able to inherit any of these. It amounted to the legal death of the family. John appears however to have managed to hold on to both land and possessions, as the Assession Rolls of 1521 show, and when he died a few years later his son, Thomas inherited these. In 1607 the attainder was officially reversed and the family honour restored.

We learn of Nicholas Daniel, an infamous vicar of this parish in Tudor times, from the account of a certain John Chapel who had been appointed to pay the wages of this recalcitrant priest and who reported that, *'Daniel was married and had a woman conversant with him and was vicar of this parish by the space of one and a half years and never resident in the said parish but was a common preacher and an unquiet person and passed from place to place never resident upon the said benefice nor never kept hospitality there.'* You will be pleased to know that Daniel was deservedly deprived of his post in 1554.

The next comprehensive written record of the village appeared in 1558 when Elizabeth I decreed that the church should register all births, marriages and burials within the parish in a bound volume to be kept in the church. In these Parish Records we have everyone's name and age, but nothing of their background or where they lived. We learned that we could estimate the total population of the village at any one time by taking the number of baptisms over a ten year period, calculating the average for one year and then multiplying this by 38 - though why this should be I have no idea. Working on this theory and taking the ten years from 1558-1568, St Teath's population in Elizabethan times appears to have been just under 500. Most of the houses would have been clustered around the church with a number of scattered farmsteads in the surrounding area.

In 1569 the St Teath Muster list gives us a slightly clearer picture of the inhabitants. It was at a time when there was a serious threat of invasion by the Spanish, who had landed in several places on the Cornish coast. A check was ordered on all local communities to see how many men would be available if needed to form a sort of Home Guard. Lists were compiled of the names and numbers of men and horses in the village, whether the men were 'able', (that is between the ages of 16 and 60), and the arms that each could provide. The St Teath Muster lists 96 men, only half of whom are classed as 'able', so today's preponderance of older people in the village seems to have had a long history. The Cornish were renowned for their archery, but some of the St Teath men appear to have had arrows but no bow and some had neither bow nor arrows. It is notable that there were only two harquebussiers (firearms) in the entire parish. It is probably fortunate that the Spanish did not choose to land at Port Gaverne and advance on St Teath.

A hundred years later the Hearth Tax Returns of 1662 provide a rough idea of the extent of housing in the village. King Charles II, the newly restored monarch, needed a regular income, so a tax was levied on householders, charging them one shilling for each fireplace or stove in the house. These returns are therefore the first record of the number and size of houses in the area. They list the names of householders and the number of hearths in each house. They also show those families exempt from the charge due to poverty or the very low value of their house. The St Teath Tax Returns show that there were approximately 120 houses in St

Teath at that time, only three of which had more than three fireplaces and two of which had fallen down. A further 41 households were not chargeable under the Act. It is clear therefore that the majority of the inhabitants at that time lived in very basic conditions and that there were few properties of any size within the village.

The population in this period (1685–1695) was about 570, hardly any increase from the previous century. There are an unusually high number of burials recorded in the year 1687, mostly in the summer months, which could have been due to the plague, which still recurred at intervals throughout this century. Or it is possible that a bad harvest had led to malnutrition. The village would be entirely dependent on the local harvest, so as the population grew, malnutrition would have been a bigger problem and the weakest would die in greater numbers. So the population would increase and then fall back on a regular basis, keeping it fairly stable throughout the centuries.

The village continued through the 1700s much as before, the number of houses and population remaining roughly the same, with the majority of St Teath men being employed as agricultural labourers on local farms or in the quarry at Delabole. When we reach the 1800s our picture of the village becomes much more detailed and records abound in the form of Tythe maps, census returns, Directories etc. The census of 1821 shows that the population had leapt to 991 people, but that they were still living in the same 150 houses where centuries earlier half that number had lived. Most of the men still worked as farm labourers, with a fair number of quarrymen working at Delabole and some miners working at Treburgett Mine. There were also three village blacksmiths, nine stonemasons, three shopkeepers and a straw-bonnet maker, among others. For almost thirty years in the mid 1800s the census describes large numbers of men as *'Miner. Out of labour'*, as Treburgett mine lay idle. Two families with ten children between them, plus two widows and a widower are all recorded as living in the Poor House (the present Community Centre) in 1851. These were hard times indeed.

The reopening of Treburgett Mine in 1869 brought increased prosperity to the village with jobs for almost 200 men, women and children. This is reflected in the number of tradesmen catering for villagers' needs: there were now four general stores plus a butcher's shop, a flour dealer, a milliner and a stay-maker (making corsets), in addition to the two publicans, three blacksmiths and numerous shoemakers and tailors. Moreover the restoration of the church building would have provided work for the masons and carpenters until its completion in 1879.

Once the mine closed the population fell once again and remained steady at around 600 throughout most of the 1900s with very little new building, apart from the development of council houses in Tetha Dene and Trevilley Lane in the 1940s. The first real change to the shape and population of the village did not come until the

1970s with the building of Valley View estate with its forty houses. then almost twenty years later the fifty-eight bungalows on neighbouring Trehannick Close. Since then the number of dwellings has continued to increase with those at Brambleside and The Meadows and bungalows dotted around the village. There are now almost 500 houses but the total population is only about 800, showing how small most households are. The average household for the entire village is now about 1.5 people per house, whereas in Victorian times it was almost 7 in what would have been much smaller houses. The good old days?

On walks around St Teath Mrs Chesher taught us how to 'read' buildings and to identify the oldest cottages by their heavy chimney stacks, thick cob walls and small windows, often with vestigial hood mouldings.

One of the oldest cottages on the 'Island' by the church

Examples of these old houses are : *Stout Cottage* next to the White Hart, several of the cottages beyond the Post Office including *Greystones* and most of the cottages round the 'Island' by the church, including *Poplars* and *Acre Bena on* Carkeen Lane. *Greystones* is a particularly interesting building dating from the 1600s when it was an ale house and later a coaching inn, *The Old White Hart*.

Greystones – The Old White Hart

We learned to look for later attempts to 'gentrify' these old cottages by adding 18th century facades (as on the present Churchtown Café building) and even later Victorian additions of decorative ridge tiles on roofs and sash windows with tripartite panes.

Our History Society was privileged to make visits to several interesting properties in the area. At *Vicarage Farm*, which had been St Teath Church's vicarage from the 13th century until 1821, we saw the outer round wall housing the projection staircase and many other original features. We were able to read Terriers describing the house over time and showing the architectural developments over the centuries. In 1680 it was described as having '*Hall, kitchen and 2 chambers and a handsomely earthed floor.* ' We were shown where Mr Worden had found the 12th century font in 1976 and we were very interested to hear that some historians thought it likely that the church silver and treasures, which must have belonged to such an important mediaeval church, may have been buried somewhere on vicarage land to prevent their being plundered by the Puritan mobs. We resisted the urge to start digging. We also visited the beautiful Tudor manors of *Tretawne*, near St Kew Highway and *Pengenna* at Trelill, the latter being a unusual example of a three-storey house of that period.

We undertook to 'beat the bounds' – to walk the parish boundary. We divided the walk into manageable chunks and allocated each section to a couple of members, who were responsible for contacting landowners for permission to trespass on their property and then for undertaking a trial run to make sure their section was in fact navigable to people of a certain age. Attempting to follow the directions of a document entitled: '*A Record of ye circuit of ye Boundes and Lymites of the pish of St Tethe vewed and scene by the Minister and pishioners there Annoque domini 1613',* we decided it was not strictly necessary to beat one of our members every time we reached a significant point on the boundary to ensure they did not forget, as was once the custom. Starting at what the document called *'Nuell Mill'* and *'going up along by ye hedge upright to ye Long Stone in John Slogget's ground ptinge between Lanteglos and St Teath and soe bounding along by ye highway till it come to the head of Castlegow ground...'* Gallantly led by our vicar, Rev Michael Pearce who sported his scarlet hiking socks and waved the large crucifix, worn around his neck, to ward off any rampaging bullocks we encountered, we bounded along through fields and woods, out towards the sea and along the coast for miles, noting that the names of many of these farms and hamlets had changed little in 400 years. We were stunned by the beauty of the scenery and the unbelievable length of the parish boundary.

Getting around the county in those early days was far from easy. We have seen how the importance of St Teath church in mediaeval times led to a vast network of footpaths linking the village with all outlying areas and how many of these footpaths have developed into today's roads. Roads in Cornwall however were unfit for wheels of any kind until well into the 1700s and most travel and transport was by sea. Any road travel was mainly on horseback and it was not until the mid-1700s that turnpikes were built enabling horse-drawn stage-coaches to provide transport links between the main towns. The very first turnpike road in Cornwall ran from Launceston to Truro and came via St Teath. It followed the route which the 95 bus takes today: along the present A39 from Camelford, turning up the hill by Knights Mill, through the village, left by the clock through Whitewell and Trelill to St Kew Highway then on to Wadebridge, St Columb and Truro. (The road through the Allen Valley linking Knights Mill with St Kew Highway was not built until 1838). The two *White Hart Inns*: the present pub and *Greystones* (with only two inns in the village it could surely not have been beyond the wit of man to think of a different name for one of them?) were coaching inns at this time, where the stagecoach would change horses before the last leg of their journey, which for some travellers could have been all the way from London. It would have been a hazardous and tortuous journey and it was customary to make your will before undertaking to travel to London from Cornwall.

The Local History Society continued with Joanna Mattingley enlightening us on many fascinating aspects of Church History. When the demise of the group finally came, I determined to make a serious effort to follow up Mrs Chesher's suggestion that we might like to write a parish history. When friends realised this was my plan they kindly gave me an assortment of old photos and documents (if any of these were intended as loans rather than donations, I apologise and now is the time to claim them back.) I have given numerous talks to local groups and societies on local history always assuring people that a book was on its way. This, at long last, is that book.

Chapter Twelve

Reminiscences

When I first began compiling this story of St Teath's past, I was lucky enough to meet and become good friends with several elderly residents of the village who have sadly since gone on, but who had lived most, if not all, of their lives here in St Teath. They remembered the early days of the 1900s well and were eager to talk about them, so for me piecing together an authentic picture of life in the village in the last century was a very rewarding and enjoyable experience.

Our neighbour, Mrs Cocks had moved to her cottage in Whitewell from Teague Terrace in the Square just after World War II and when I got to know her in 1975 her lifestyle had hardly changed at all since then. It was only the previous year that Mrs Cocks had consented to have a sink installed and water piped into the house. She still had no bathing facilities or a lavatory of any kind. "Can't be doing with all that upheaval at my age. I be quite 'appy as I be," she would tell me, as she threw the contents of her slop bucket out over the garden each morning. The dear lady used to complain about the cost of her rent which was 1/6 a week – one shilling and sixpence, which even at that time would hardly have bought a loaf of bread. Her kindly landlord had bought Cocks Cottage many years earlier, with Mrs Cocks as a sitting tenant. He had not increased the rent since taking over the place and had tried in vain to install a bathroom of some kind and improve the state of the cottage for the old lady. A gully went diagonally across the middle of the living room and ran with water when there was a heavy downpour. Mrs Cocks' only means of cooking and heating was the open fire in the old, black range in the kitchen/living room But her cottage was always cosy, warm and welcoming.

Mrs Cocks told me how in the 1920s and 30s one of the highlights of the summer had been the August Bank Holiday Monday trip to spend the day on Tregardock beach Groups of villagers would walk the 3 miles or so to the beach, pushing their picnics and babies in wheelbarrows through the village to the Delabole road then down towards Treligga, across the fields and down the bumpy path to the beach. They would stay there all day, making a fire using furze-bushes as fuel to warm up the pasties and boil the water for tea. Then as the light faded, they would walk back with the smallest children asleep in their parents' arms. There were also the Sunday School outings to Polzeath in wagons and wagonettes, when they all had to get out and walk whenever they went up or down hills.

Mrs Best, Mrs Cocks' closest friend, whom she had known for over fifty years but whom she never addressed by her Christian name, would visit once a week without fail and entertain us with more stories of the past. She told us how Mrs Cocks' late husband used to shoot trout in the stream and throw the fish-heads on the garden as fertiliser, a practice which clearly offended Mrs Best's delicate nose. When she realised how eager I was to know everything about the village's past, she took to writing things down when she thought of them in her beautifully neat handwriting. She recalled how in the days before mains water reached St Teath there had been at least nine or ten windless pumps at various points in the village but that the water from the pump at Whitewell was considered the best. The Gabriel family who lived in Cobb Cottage next to the pump had thirteen children, spaced out at yearly intervals and Mrs Gabriel used to persuade a couple of strong lads from the village to carry endless pails of water from the pump up into her cottage and reward them with *half* a sweet each.

Mrs Best's memories of the Second World War were of being issued with gas masks and of having to put blackout material up to the windows every night or be liable for a fine from the strict ARP wardens who patrolled the village each evening after dark. A Home Guard was formed mostly from men who had served in the First World War and they used to guard vital installations. She recalled bombs and incendiary bombs being dropped in a field at China Downs by an enemy plane which was being chased by the RAF. A British light aircraft made a forced landing in a field off Trevilley Lane; the pilot was not injured and many villagers went over to see the wrecked plane. She also remembered a coachload of evacuees arriving from the London area and being given a tea in the Church Hall, before being billeted with those families who had spare bedrooms. Many of the children stayed here for nearly two years, settled into village life very happily and were sorry to leave their adopted families.

Others who arrived in the village during the War were Italian prisoners of war who were housed in a camp on the outskirts and sent to work on farms in the area. They were, by all accounts, made very welcome and treated kindly by both villagers and the farmers for whom they worked. They attended local dances and the Regal Cinema in Delabole and for many this was one of the happiest periods of their lives.

Both Mrs Cocks and Mrs Best hinted occasionally at a darker episode in St Teath's history but were clearly reluctant to go into any detail, until one day Mrs Cocks announced, "I think ee'd best go talk to Mrs Burt. 'er knowed all about they things." So off I went, my head full of questions but feeling slightly apprehensive about approaching the lady who probably had no idea who I was. I need not have worried. Once I announced that Mrs Cocks had sent me, Mrs Burt welcomed me in, gave me tea and chatted willingly for hours. She had lived next door to the cottage where St Teath's only recorded murder had taken place and she remembered it well, despite the fifty years that had passed since this tragic event. This was the desperately sad tale she told me:

It was sometime in 1920 when Mrs Osborne and her daughter, Trennie came to live in Union Row at the top of Treroosal Road. They moved here from Trebarwith House, where Mrs Osborne had been housekeeper.

Trennie was a strikingly beautiful girl with long tresses of dark hair which reached down to her waist. She was well liked by all the villagers, although her mother was a proud woman who did not mix with the neighbours and had no close friends. " 'er thought 'er was too good for we," commented Mrs Burt.

Trennie soon became friends with Annie Wallis, the daughter of the publican in the White Hart Inn and Trennie worked there occasionally to earn a little money. In the early months of 1923 it became apparent to all who knew her that Trennie was pregnant, although no mention of this was ever made openly. Mrs Osborne remained as aloof as ever. Trennie was just fifteen years old.

On Easter Sunday Trennie was taken ill in church and Mrs Kingdon, the vicar's wife took her home. Mrs Osborne refused Mrs Kingdon's offer to call a doctor, ushered Trennie inside and shut the door. When Trennie was next seen in the village she was no longer pregnant, but was clearly unwell. There was no sign of a baby. There was great consternation among the women of the village and eventually two doctors, one from Camelford and one from St Tudy came to the Osborne's house, After their visit Mrs Osborne appeared to lose control and rushed around the house, closing windows and locking doors.

The next day all was quiet at the Osborne's cottage. The only sign of life was their spaniel dog who sat up at the bedroom window looking out and whining. When the whole day passed without anyone opening the door or answering the neighbour's calls, Mrs Osborne's brother, Aaron Ede was alerted. That evening he and a friend, Mr Giles, decided to break into the cottage via a back-bedroom window. They were confronted with a dreadful scene: Trennie was lying dead on the bed with her throat slit and a knife at her side. Mrs Osborne lay dead on the same bed with a stab wound to her throat and surrounded by blood-soaked towels. It seemed clear that Mrs Osborne had killed her daughter and then taken her own life. The body of the baby was never found although police made an extensive search of the area, digging up all the gardens nearby. It was suggested that the body may have been thrown down one of the shafts at the recently abandoned Treburgett mine, but that is only speculation.

The funeral was a particularly sad event for villagers who had become very fond of Trennie and the church was packed for the service. Mrs Osborne's coffin was left outside in the churchyard, since she had committed the two crimes of murder – the double murder of both her daughter and the baby? - and suicide. Trennie's uncle had the headstone in their memory erected in St Teath cemetery.

That was the tragic tale, as recounted to me by Mrs Burt, the Osborne's neighbour. I researched further and discovered in the Cornish Guardian of 27th April 1923, between ads for *Gill's Charming Millinery – Hats for 9/11* and *Lennard's children's double-wearing, wet-resisting shoes,* a report entitled: *Terrible Double Tragedy – St Teath woman's Mad Act.* It told how Mrs Osborne, widow

of Henry Osborne, a naval man who had lost his life at sea many years ago, had murdered her daughter and then committed suicide. It went on to describe how, after the shadow of local scandal had been hanging over the pair for several weeks, an anonymous letter to the police suggesting *'a certain thing had happened'* resulted in visits from the local constable to their home on 2 or 3 days of the previous week. On Friday Mrs Osborne had failed to appear, so her brother, Mr Aaron Walter Ede went to the house several times then at midnight he and Mr Giles got a ladder and entered the back bedroom where they found the pair lying on the same bed with gashes to the throat. PC Mallet of Delabole was sent for and found two knives.

The report goes on to say an inquest was held later the same day in the Church Rooms with a jury of seven men. Annie Wallis was questioned and said that Trennie had been to see her on Thursday evening and had said people were making an awful scandal about her which was hard to bear. Annie went round to the Osborne's about 10.15 that night but the lights were out, she shouted to Trennie who said they were in bed but she would see Annie on Friday morning. When Annie went the next day the door was locked and all was quiet, she thought Trennie was ill and her mother had gone to work, leaving her in bed. When questioned, Dr Jerome of Camelford confirmed that the wound to Trennie's neck could not have been suicide and was probably done while the girl was asleep. The wound to the mother's throat was a stab through to the spinal cord. He was asked about his previous examination of Trennie but would not divulge his findings. When asked if the results of the examination were made known to the deceased and whether they were worried, he answered that they were. Then he was asked if the scandal in the village was just hearsay to which he answered, 'No'. The report's conclusion was: *'It's the woman who pays the price every time.'*

In the interests of a full account, I must add that since investigating this tragic story, I have been made aware on a number of occasions of an alternative conclusion which was not mentioned either by Mrs Burt or in the newspaper report. A descendant of one of the jurors at the inquest maintains that the identity of the father of Trennie's child was common knowledge in the village and that this man may have played a part in their deaths, but as far as I know, no evidence has ever been put forward for this version of events. Whatever the truth, it is a desperately sad story and a terrible waste of three lives.

Another fellow-enthusiast of local history was Mr Morley Treleaven, an elderly gentleman from the farm next door who had a treasure trove of anecdotes from the past and a wonderful sense of fun. Once he realised how interested I was, Morley delighted in spinning tales about the characters who had inhabited our cottage. A particular favourite was Frederick Gibbons who had come to St Teath originally to work at Treburgett Mine and who had lodged with Miss France and her aunt in our cottage. He was something of an amateur inventor and it was he who had set up a pump to pipe water to the house from our well on the far side of the farm drive. Morley told me of the day when Frederick had invited him to see his latest invention: he had attached an old gramophone with a large horn speaker to the water pipe from the well, so that when he turned on the pump the water gushed high into the air in a fountain from the speaker and as a finishing touch he had a ping-pong ball dancing on the top.

On several memorable occasions Morley would turn up on my doorstep with an armful, and sometimes a wheelbarrow full, of books, Kelly's Directories and other old local guidebooks, which he had found in a second-hand shop and was eager to share with me. He also asked me to join in with some of his exploits, such as measuring the circumference of the huge ash tree across the road, in order to calculate its age - which appeared to be over 200 years – and opening up an old adit to a mine at the top of the field behind our house. With the help of John Mewton and his digger, we removed a yard or two of topsoil in the spot where Morley reckoned the adit to be. Sure enough after ten minutes or so of digging we were thrilled to see the remains of a doorway leading downwards. The tunnel behind it had collapsed after a few yards, but along the top of the wooden door-frame was a row of coins, pennies, halfpennies, shillings and florins, all with Queen Victoria's head on them. We added a few coins of our own from the 1980s, carefully covered them all with a wooden bar and asked John to fill the hole in once more.

Mr Les Mewton, owner of Trehannick Sawmills, who lived in Hillcrest, a few minutes' walk up the lane from our cottage, had a phenomenal memory and could recall names, dates and events in great detail from over fifty years previously. On one occasion when I sat down with Les he went through every house in the village and gave me the names of everyone who lived there just after the war, and often the names of previous owners as well, just for good measure. He described the numerous shops and tradesmen and gave me an interestingly detailed account of St Teath Garage.

Tonkins' garage in the 1920s.

After the War the garage was owned by Harold Burden and his wife, Kyle, who was the village school mistress. Harold had bought the garage from Jim Hill, but it had been started in 1925 by William Tonkin, who had previously worked as a mechanic for the Coop in Delabole and had sold bikes from a wooden hut in St Teath where the bus shelter now stands. Besides doing car repairs, Harold sold petrol and paraffin and opened a shop selling cigarettes, tobacco, confectionery, soft drinks, electrical goods and bicycles.

The business provided all St Teath's drivers' needs for thirty years or so, until Harold retired and sold the garage and shop to Don Maynard who carried on the business, employing Henry Richardson as car mechanic. In 1969 Don sold the business to John Treleaven who continued to employ Henry and to sell petrol until the storage tanks proved too small for the suppliers and they refused to deliver any longer. John then demolished the old shop and garage and built a splendid new one with modern equipment and concentrated solely on repairs. The new building was opened with a magnificent village party on the premises with flashing lights and the loudest music St Teath had ever heard. John ran a thriving business until 1985 when John & Andy Noble took over and served the village well for the next 18 years. The garage finally closed in 2003 and the site was developed to provide the housing known as *Koth Karji*, 'the old garage' in Cornish.

Les told me how Daisy Stainthorpe, sister of Miss France who owned our cottage in the 1920s, had set up shop selling newspapers and paraffin in the wooden hut previously used by Mr Tonkin for his bikes. There was

Magor's butcher's shop, Mr Tucker's fishmongers and Mr Parsons sweetshop, all in what is now Central House in the Square, plus Mr & Mrs Spry's Fish & Chip shop opposite the present Churchtown café. Miss Haynes had a Milliner's shop, essential in those days when women never went out without a hat, Mr & Mrs Sloggett ran the village's first Coop store on Fore Street in the house now called *Sherwell* and Mr Smith had a carpenter's shop in *Greystones*. There was a corn store where the *Muts Cuts* house now stands and Mr George had a corn-mill at *Knights Mill*, while Mr Mewton ground corn using two large waterwheels at *Trehannick Mill.* Philip Giles, a second carpenter, lived in *Brick House* and rented the ground floor of the Community Centre as his workshop. There were cottages and piggeries on Trevilley Lane, then known as *Ducky Street*, which were demolished to make way for the flats and new houses. He remembered the blacksmith, Mr Auger who lived in *Forge Cottage*, as well as Lewis Bligh Hicks, another blacksmith who lived in The Square.

I was intrigued by the name Bligh in the blacksmith's name and Les told me he thought he may very well have been descended from the famous Captain Bligh who was born in St Teath. I had never heard of this, but Les assured me that it was true. I followed up this surprising piece of information and discovered that indeed both Gilbert's *History of Cornwall* and Lake's *Parochial History of Cornwall* gave St Teath as Captain Bligh's birthplace. However it has apparently long been a matter of contention between St Teath and St Tudy with both claiming to be the birthplace of the renowned – or notorious – captain. There is no reference to Bligh's baptism in St Teath's Parish Records, whereas St Tudy Church register has an entry in *February 1757* stating that *William Bligh, son of Charles & Margaret, together with Mary, his sister* were both baptised there on that date. We know that Bligh's family lived at some point in the ancient manor of Tinten near St Tudy, We also know that Captain Bligh died in London in 1817 aged 63, so he would have been 3 years old at the time of this baptism. It was common practice to delay the baptism of siblings and have them baptised together, so it is possible that William was indeed born in St Teath but not baptised until two or three years later when the family had moved to Tinten.

Whether we should be proud of this famous captain is also a matter of dispute. Bligh served with Captain Cook on his third voyage around the world and won praise from Cook for his conduct as Master. In 1787 he was appointed to command the *Bounty* on a voyage to Tahiti to collect breadfruit plants to take to the West Indies. On the return journey the crew mutinied and Bligh, together with 18 loyal crew members, was cast adrift in a longboat. After a journey of nearly a year and over 4,000 miles, Bligh successfully navigated his way to Timor in Indonesia and from there returned to England. He made a second voyage to Tahiti and the Caribbean two years later with two ships, successfully delivered the breadfruit and returned safely to England with no problems. He served under Nelson at the Battle of Copenhagen and was promoted to Vice-Admiral. He became governor of New South Wales in 1806 but the settlers again rebelled against his strict disciplinarian approach and the military deposed him. He returned to England, where some regarded him as a heartless tyrant but others saw him as a great hero and there is evidence of parents even naming their children after him. Could our blacksmith's name have been a relic of these times?

Another dear friend who lived on the outskirts of the village told me of the days when the North Cornwall Railway with its steam locomotives thundered along the line to Port Isaac Road station. She lived close to the track and complained that the soot from the engine had ruined her washing and sparks would often set fire to her garden, as the giant engine emerged from Trelill tunnel and steamed past her house. Port Isaac Road station had opened in 1895. This section of the line was built originally to transport fish and shellfish from Port Isaac, and the entire line ran from the harbour at Padstow to Wadebridge, then St Kew, Port Isaac Road, Delabole, Camelford, Otterham, Launceston, Halwill, Exeter, then non-stop to Waterloo. This part of the line was not built for speed, due to the steep gradient of many sections and the narrow, winding route and deep cuttings through the countryside. The rest of the line, however, must have made up for this slow start, as by the 1930s the Atlantic Coast Express did the 260 mile journey from Padstow to Waterloo in just five and a half hours. The sight and sound of the huge steam trains powering their way through the Cornish countryside must have been impressive.

It is not surprising that the residents of towns and villages were wary of having such monsters in their midst. Delabole was the only station on this stretch of line that was built in the village itself, with Camelford Station being nearly 3 miles from the town, Otterham Station 2 miles from the village and Port Isaac Road a whole 4 miles away from the port. I once asked the stationmaster at Bodmin Road station, (today's Bodmin Parkway) why they had built the station so far from the town itself. His answer was that I should be grateful they had built it near the track. (It was actually built to serve the Lanhydrock estate).

Sadly, following the Beeching Report in 1964, the North Cornwall line closed for good, barely a decade before we arrived. How lovely it would have been to walk up the road to the station, 10 minutes away, and been able to catch the train to Waterloo.

The coming of the railway and its eventual demise just 70 years later makes only a tiny mark on the long timeline of St Teath's history stretching back nearly two thousand years. Time is a difficult concept to grasp in a village, the routes into which were established in the Middle Ages and have changed little since then, where farmsteads can trace their origins to a time before the Norman conquest and where the heart of its community has remained on the very same spot since Celtic times. Past and present merge and time means little. So when I reflect on the fact that I started planning this book in 1975 and a glance at the calendar today as I write this final paragraph tells me the year is now 2020, it comes as no surprise that it has taken the whole of forty-five years to complete. As Mr Spry informed that impatient commuter all those years ago, "Nothing moves that fast down 'ere, me 'ansome."

ACKNOWLEDGEMENTS

I owe a debt of gratitude to so many people, without whom this book would never have been written. Sadly many of them are no longer with us, but their knowledge and tales of the village's past have helped to enrich its present. Heartfelt thanks to Mrs Veronica Chesher, Mrs Cocks, Mrs Best, Mrs Burt, Les Mewton, Morley Treleaven, Winnie Leverton, Lorraine Jasper and the many other friends and villagers whose support and encouragement have been invaluable.

The photos on pages 19,50,52,59,65,70,107 and on the back cover are by kind permission of Brenda Burnard. The illustration on page 39 is from *Popular Romances of the West of England 1891*.

BIBLIOGRAPHY

Celtic Christianity of Cornwall   by T.Taylor (1916)
History of Trigg Minor by Sir John Maclean (1879)
A brief Guide to the Church of St Tetha by Rev W.J.C. Armstrong (1932)
Old Cornish Crosses by Arthur Langdon (1893)
Cornish Characters and Strange Events by S. Baring-Gould (1908)
Popular Romances of the West of England by Robert Hunt (1891)
Mines and Miners of Cornwall by A.K. Hamilton Jenkins
The Wesleys in Cornwall by John Pearce (1964)
A History of Cornwall Vol II by Hitchins & Drew (1824)
Lake's Parochial History of the County of Cornwall (1867)
A Parochial History of Cornwall Vol IV by Davies Gilbert (1838)
The History of Port Isaac and Port Quin   by Dr Frederick Trevan (unpublished)
Kelly's Directories; Cornish Glebe Terriers; St Teath Church Logbook ; St Teath CP School Logbooks